nva

the STORR

UNFOLDING LANDSCAPE

Compiled and edited by Angus Farquhar

Luath Press Ltd
Edinburgh
www.luath.co.uk

First Published 2005

The publisher acknowledges subsidy
from the Scottish Arts Council

Q Scottish
Arts Council

towards the publication of this volume.

We printed by kind permission of publisher Carcanet Press Ltd.

The paper used in this book is recyclable.
Printed on Revive Matt – made from a minimum
of 75% de-inked post consumer waste and Kaskad.

Printed and bound by
J Thomson Colour Printers Ltd, Glasgow

Edit team:
nva: Angus Farquhar, Elspeth McLachlan,
Ellen Gibbons, Skye-media

Luath Press Ltd: Gavin MacDougall, Tim West

Designed by Graphical House:
Daniel Ibbotson, Graeme Johnson, Colin Raeburn

Contents

To David Bryant
– because you have what it takes

nva is an environmental arts charity based in Scotland. Founded in 1992, the company has built a powerful reputation through the delivery of temporary and permanent artworks across Europe. These include *The Hidden Gardens*, the award winning sanctuary garden in Glasgow, and a number of renowned interventions in both urban and natural locations.

www.nva.org.uk

Extract from *An Cuilithionn*
reproduced by kind permission
of Carcanet Press Ltd

An Cuilithionn

Somhairle MacGill-Eain

Fada, cian fada, fada air faire
chi mi tulgadh a' Chuilithinn chràcaich,
thar marannan dòlais, thar mòinteach àmhghair,
chi mi geal shuaimhneas nan stuadh bheann àrda.

Có seo, có seo oidhche dhona,
có seo a' coiseachd air a' mhonadh?
Ceumannan spioraid ri mo thaobh
agus ceumannan ciùin mo ghaoil,

ceumannan, ceumannan air na sléibhtean,
monmhar cheumannan ag éirigh:
ceumannan fiata, ceumannan ciùine,
ceumannan èalaidh socair mùinte.

Có seo, có seo oidhche dunaidh,
có seo a' coiseachd air a' mhullach?
Tannasg eanchairine luime nochdte,
fuar ri aognaidheachd an torchairt.

Có seo, có seo oidhche 'n spioraid?
Chan eil ach tannasg lom cridhe,
manadh leis fhéin a' falbh a' smaointinn,
cliabh feòil-rùiste air an aonach.

Có seo, có seo oidhche chridhe?
Chan eil ach an nì do-ruighinn,
an samhla a chunnaic an t-anam,
Cuilithionn ag éirigh thar mara.

Có seo, có seo oidhche 'n anama
a' leantainn fiaradh an leòis fhalbhaich?
Chan eil, chan eil ach am falbhan
a' sireadh a' Chuilithinn thar fairge.

Có seo, có seo oidhche chinne?
Chan eil ach samhla an spioraid,
anam leis fhéin a' falbh air sléibhtean,
ag iargain a' Chuilithinn 's e 'g éirigh.

Extract from *The Cuillin*
reproduced by kind permission
of Carcanet Press Ltd

The Cuillin

Sorley MacLean

Far, far distant, far on a horizon,
I see the rocking of the antlered Cuillin,
beyond the seas of sorrow, beyond the morass of agony,
I see the white felicity of the high-
towered mountains.

Who is this, who is this on a bad night,
who is this walking on the moorland?
The steps of a spirit by my side
and the soft steps of my love:

footsteps, footsteps on the mountains,
murmur of footsteps rising,
quiet footsteps, gentle footsteps,
stealthy mild restrained footsteps.

Who is this, who is this on a night of woe,
who is this, walking on the summit?
The ghost of a bare naked brain,
cold in the chill of vicissitude.

Who is this, who is this in the night of the spirit?
It is only the naked ghost of a heart,
a spectre going alone in thought,
a skeleton naked of flesh on the mountain.

Who is this, who is this in the night of the heart?
It is the thing that is not reached,
the ghost seen by the soul,
a Cuillin rising over the sea.

Who is this, who is this in the night of the soul,
following the veering of the fugitive light?
It is only, it is only the journeying one
seeking the Cuillin over the ocean.

Who is this, who is this in the night of mankind?
It is only the ghost of the spirit,
a soul alone going on mountains,
longing for the Cuillin that is rising.

Angus Farquhar
Tower Ridge, Ben Nevis
Noel Williams

Foreground

Angus Farquhar

Storr winter panorama
Simon Corder

In 2002 a Creative Scotland award set me off to walk some of the greatest surviving pilgrimage routes in the world. From the grey-blue glacier of Gaumukh at the source of the Ganges, to the ancient Camino de Santiago de Compostela, Galicia; the stations of the cross at La Verna, Italy and finally to Mount Sinai in Egypt.

A mountain sacred to Christians, Muslims and Jews, Mount Sinai stands as a shared symbol of such significance that differing layers of human history and belief are able to lie invisibly interwoven on its surface. Every night, surrounded by miles of desert, thousands of people with hand held torches walk towards dawn, an uncoiling line of flickering energy, snaking upwards with single intent. An ascent allows each person to move through the same physical territory, yet experience it from radically different perspectives. On the night I was there I heard over 20 distinct languages being spoken.

Coming out of this great ritual act, which has continued for over 1,200 years, is the idea that we rarely see things as they actually are, but rather as we imagine they are. After *The Path* – the **nva** landscape work in Glen Lyon – it was clear that of the 5,000 people who walked the route, there were hugely varying responses to the work. Reading a natural landscape is therefore a complex undertaking – how to begin understanding the accretions that have built up over time to reveal its underlying reality.

The islands of Raasay and Skye are particular in having the unique voice of Sorley MacLean to articulate their special character in the world. While his words are specific to a place, they also speak to a wider human condition, a commonality of emotional need and aspiration. At heart his poems are a celebration of the power of the creative act itself. Trees, ridges, summits and other natural formations take on new meanings, creating a transparency to a parallel world to ours, full of hope, terror, beauty and loss; geological and cultural history intermingling as vision and fact, deep time with recent time, beyond physical constraints.

In this light, we see landscapes defined as much by absence as by what is there. Natural forces so powerful that their impact still echoes in great rock falls, thousands of years after the last ice age. The strange marriage of violence and stillness. The work also points to the unseen, what is embedded in the earth and stone, the power of language to reclaim and restore.

Sine Gillespie describes heritage as '*Doing time somewhere with Your eyes. Your ears. Your hands. Your feet. Your heart. Your soul.*' This collection of essays reflects a range of perspectives by writers whose depth of response, powers of observation, and insight imply the same patience and willingness to wait for answers. They help to articulate the complexity of the forms and meanings that underpin what we know simply as *nature*.

Background
Seona Reid

nva occupies a unique place both in the arts landscape and in the physical landscape – and, of course, what is exciting about the company is its ability to bring these two landscapes together in some of the most profound site-specific work in Europe today.

Over the years, of course, both the art and the landscape which **nva** has brought together has changed and evolved.

I arrived back in Scotland in 1990 to become Director of the Scottish Arts Council and one of my first events was *The Second Coming*, devised and performed by Test Department Productions at the St Rollox Locomotive Works in Springburn in Glasgow. It was a huge event in every way, taking over an entire locomotive yard; it included a battery of drums whose sound, demanding and uncompromising, filled the vast space, and also involved 50 performers moving in, under and over an array of trains, cranes and other mechanised objects.

The whole conception was fabulously ambitious, from the theme – the romanticisation of our industrial heritage – eloquently drawn by Neal Ascherson, to the awe inspiring location so redolent of Glasgow's industrial history.

In 1992, **nva** evolved out of Test Department and the next big site-specific event I attended was *Stormy Waters* in 1995. Again the theme of Glasgow's past was a starting point and the location was the fabulous Meadowside Granary on the north side of the Clyde, overlooking the Kvaerner Govan Shipyards, the last working shipyard on the river's upper reaches. Huge projected images, sound and text animated the site, manipulated by artists on five continents and then represented on large screens via the internet. The work juxtaposed the old Glasgow, with its civic grandeur, historical class structures and institutions, with the forms of political and social engagement which were becoming possible through internet and digital technologies.

In 1998, *The Secret Sign* was the first project to use the natural landscape. I remember climbing into a minibus in central Glasgow one May evening and hurtling through country roads to arrive at a muddy field somewhere in Stirlingshire. Issued with green waders and ex-military hard hats, we were led waist high in water down the river in Finnich Glen. As we waded through the river, the gorge, redolent with its history and tales of witches and Covenanters, was animated with coloured light which flitted across the rock face; with haunting soundscapes, distant voices and the call of birds; with the unnerving appearance and disappearance of figures with torches and guns above us in the pitch dark. Every now and then a large bird of prey, sitting motionless on a rock, would blink. We arrived in the natural amphitheatre opposite the Devil's Pulpit. The scene exploded and a hawk emerged from the hands of a human silhouette etched against fire and swooped low over our heads, the whoosh of its wings in our ears. There was no applause – how could there be?

In 2000, *The Path* was the next major work in the natural landscape – an extraordinary four mile walk into one of the most beautiful glens in highland Scotland. *The Path* made connections between Scottish highland culture and the highland culture of the Himalayas, bringing Sherpa guides and musicians from Nepal to work on the piece. Following an old peat track, light and sound played with the natural features of the glen and the vestiges of old human habitation. We walked past derelict shielings from which the soft sound of a Gaelic lullaby could be heard; past a huge boulder tied down with rope, which groaned as if straining to be free.

In the far distance, fires burned, faint bagpipes were heard, rocks seemed to move – or were they figures? On a hilltop a huge cairn sheltered a Tibetan singer who performed an unforgettable lament. Already a landscape full of beauty and redolent with history, Glen Lyon, through **nva**'s poetic intervention, became a metaphor for ways in which human beings, wherever they are, make sense of the land on which they depend and build profound relationships with it.

The company has consistently produced unique, memorable, and very personal experiences, rooted in geology, in history and in national cultures, which are so sensitively handled, so open and generous, that one's own memories, emotions and spirituality have room to connect. The work is always built on respect – respect for the landscape in which it locates, respect for the cultures it seeks to interpret and respect for those who witness it.

Walking, Drifting & Meandering

Peter McCaughey

1 *Society of the Spectacle*
(Black & Red) p1

Every year the course in Environmental Art at Glasgow School of Art starts
with an introduction for the new students to the radical ideas of the Situationists,
an influential group of thinkers, artists and writers mainly active in the late
sixties. The Situationists used the *dérive* (literally the 'drift') as a tool to
re-negotiate the city.

The introduction to the *dérive* begins by putting a plate onto a map of inner
city Glasgow and drawing a line around it. This makes a nice circle, as you can
imagine, that passes through supermarkets, brick walls, parks, police stations,
disused property, public and private space. The students are then split into two
groups and are invited to walk the circle, with one group travelling clockwise
and the other anti-clockwise. Their aim is to keep to the line in so far as they
can. The following week, after they have recovered, or been released, they head
up to Skye on a three day field trip.

This comparison between cityscape and landscape offers a great opportunity
to reflect on how much our immediate environment shapes everything about
us. At first we don't quite know what to do with ourselves in this perfect place.
A lot of the students who respond to the things that are dysfunctional, broken
and unloved within the city, seem lost facing the Cuillins. Richard Dawkins'
theory on the uncaring universe comes clearly into focus facing this amazing
landscape – it doesn't need us. It certainly doesn't need us sitting there on a
sunny day, by a cliff top or a beachhead, trying to paint and draw things.
Whereas the City, in all its fucked up, neon glory, does need us, if only to
point out where it's all going wrong.

In addressing the conditions that create 'alienated living', Guy Debord,
self-proclaimed leader of SI (Situationist International), heavily critiqued
the spectacle and wrote on how we might devise strategies to re-connect to
ourselves and each other, particularly within city living.

'In societies where modern conditions of production prevail, all of life presents
itself as an immense accumulation of spectacles. Everything that was directly
lived has moved away into a representation.'[1]

The 'spectacle' was seen as an alienating force within modern life. He felt it diminished us, infantilised us, left us in a continual state of awe. Yet perhaps this sense of spectacle, of the epic, has a fundamental role within our culture and our art. Kept in balance, in carefully choreographed moments, it can capture an orchestrated transcendence. Here the 'wow' factor is not an end in itself, but contributes to the possibility of a genuine epiphany, a man-made sublime. In a culture of a vast 'accumulation of spectacles' (film, TV, advertising), the spectacle can also be used against itself, to neutralise its seductive, enervating force.

Over the last decade and a half, there has been a prominent element of the spectacle present in much of **nva**'s work. The sheer scale, the dramatic revelations, the use of sound and light have on occasion conspired to overwhelm.

Yet the practice has also travelled and mutated over the years, on a journey from its early beginnings in promenade performance art/theatre, to its latest manifestation. In **nva**'s nature based work a unique form is emerging that seems to enter relatively uncharted territory in the history of either theatre or art. In some of the earlier productions, the balance between the spectacle and the content slipped in a way that no doubt Debord would have felt lessened the space for the individual to have ownership over, rather than 'be owned by', the work.

I have a strong impression that *The Storr* brings with it an evolution away from the dramatic impact of earlier work, in a search for a new balance between the intimate and the grand, the private and the panoramic.

In his fantastic publication *Landscape and Memory*, Simon Schama talks in his introduction of the historians who guarded the memories of particular landscapes at particular times:

'Each one believed that an understanding of landscape's past traditions was a source of illumination for the present and future… They waxed passionate about their favourite places because they believed they could redeem the hollowness of contemporary life.'

In a way, I think a significant part of what I would classify as **nva**'s 'landscape works, *The Secret Sign* (Devil's Pulpit, 1998), and *The Path* (Glen Lyon, 2000), operates on this level, of the sharing of a passion for these hidden treasures, these special places.

It's one of my favourite things to hear artists, or anyone for that matter, discuss what they strongly react to. At its best, this is what cultural dialogue is all about, the sharing of our journeys and visions, as well as our dark thoughts and fears, our intense beliefs and our moments of connection, our sublime experiences or rare epiphanies. Very often, in the visual arts, it's that ineffable stuff we just can't find the words to describe.

I am struggling to catch and frame the memory of such a moment I had on *The Path* half way up Glen Lyon. I had come to the top of the walk and paused to turn round. There below me unfolded the entire work, like an aerial map of a landing strip at night, except instead of straight lines there were sinuous twists and curves and a feeling of an ancient geometry that was formed from the lights that had guided our path. Of course the view on the way up had hinted at this but the act of looking down was truly breathtaking, as all the fragments of the experience on the ascent coalesced into a meaningful whole.

This is the 'spectacular' moment which for me gifts this overview; this moment where we are simultaneously at the centre of our experience and have a sense of being outside it. In thinking about how the ascent offers this vantage point upon our own path, there is a link to the strange state of 'out of body' experiences, accessed through becoming conscious of the act of dreaming whilst still asleep – those moments of having an objective eye on ourselves. (The recipe is simple. If you become conscious of yourself dreaming – look at your hands in the dream).

In cultural terms it is like the 'something' in us that retains the ability to be 'external' and removed from immersion within any given process, be it theatre, TV, narrative text, pictorial depiction. This consciousness demands that we stop buying into the illusory power of the given medium and step out of the 'dream' to connect to reality. The suspension of suspension of disbelief.

The Storr, like *The Path*, seems to offer us a strange conjunction of both possibilities. On one hand the balance of the arduous ascent and navigation of dangerous territory will keep our minds focused in the present, denying that

Extract from *A Point in Time*
reproduced by kind permission
of Carcanet Press Ltd

internal reflection, that illusory projection, gifted through the concentrated immobility that in cinema and theatre allows us to 'immerse'.

On the other hand I can imagine that the power of this very same physical immersion in the landscape – actually being there – is what opens up our shutters on perception, so that we can journey internally with what we are offered. You can trace this 'living embodiment' of an artwork from roots in the 'promenade' aspect of early theatre, back to those ancient gatherings where a high priestess would orchestrate an orgiastic ritual with the fornicating audience. On those occasions it was actually believed that at the high point of the ceremony, a moment of life-changing transcendence would occur and a spirit would descend and occupy the soul.

This oscillation between the seemingly internal, and apparently external, the mind and the body, is connected beautifully in Hugh MacDiarmid's poem, 'A Point in Time'.

Now you can understand how stars and hearts are one with another

And how there can nowhere be an end, nowhere a hindrance

How the boundless dwells perfect and undivided in the spirit

How each part can be infinitely great and infinitely small?

How the utmost extension is but a point, and how

Light, harmony, movement, power

All identical, all separate, and all united are life.

The Path Diaries

Angus Farquhar

In April and May 2000 **nva** staged a major environmental
animation in Glen Lyon, Perthshire after looking at 40
locations across Scotland. A walked route at night,
it was seen by 5,000 people. The following represents
snatches of thoughts and commentary written in
'real time' over the two years of development.

previous: *The Path*
Alan McAteer

this page:*The Path*
Al Bell

Ecstatic after drive to Glen Lyon, take the high road over Ben Lawers, a deep evening sunlight with strange out of focus clouds and spreading rays backlighting some magnificent peaks on the way through. I drove slowly, the quality of the landscape sets me tingling – tomorrow will reveal whether the feeling extends deeper into the Glen. Realise I could find the most amazing landscapes in Scotland, with huge peaks ringing a perfect valley or high waterfall, but if the weather goes wrong, you could lose everything. Perhaps I should be getting more pragmatic and working out what things to put togetherwhen the big panoramic animation might not be available.

*

First walk in Gleann an Eig, which runs from height down into Glen Lyon; up past exposed rocky pools, blossoming trees and a huge split rock resembling two upright hands, side by side. Further on to broken down shielings and a small knoll deep in the Glen, remote and detached from the start point. The drover's road leads back down the other side of the burn through powerful outcrops of rockfall and cliff faces in miniature – an almost Japanese quality, as trees cling to the vertical surfaces. The idea unfolds around small close elements revealed stage by stage, involving a single route with diversions to special points of interest.

*

Overcast and cloudy, nearly pitch black night, I sense the vaguest outlines of trees, rocks and crags against the sky. On the route with DB [David Bryant, lighting designer] who has chronic asthma, we have one fading torch between us. It felt threatening and malevolent. The eyes unable to see what the ears hear, the fear of things hidden and unreadable.

*

How can we inspire a deeper reading of this landscape? One where human values and ideas collide with or embrace the physical territory. The artificial construct will be to imply that the route has been chosen to specifically reveal important features which are then marked with ritual or votive offerings. A visit to Akong Rinpoche, head lama of Samye Ling Tibetan Centre, he introduces the notion of how people magnetise a place, which then loops energy back to the person. A starting point for understanding the positioning of power places.

Get the keys for a production cottage, Balmenoch, at the foot of the route,
empty except for a single calendar hung on the wall, three entries for 1998:

April	first cuckoo
August	Killin highland games
October	first snow

*

So much of my life is about finding physical activity that bombards me with
sensation. There is the benefit of keeping fit and the easy thrill of competition,
but I acknowledge a lack of stillness, somehow not using all this 'doing'
to reach gentler ground.

*

The idea is evolving of a comparison between Buddhist belief focussed around
high places and our own folk history. The easiest way to do this, to map the
ascent up the west of the burn as 'Highland' to the fording point and exploring
a 'Himalayan' perspective on the eastern descent. I commit to going on a trek
to Helambu in Nepal with Doug Scott and Samye Ling. If we are going to talk
about landscape from different traditions, what right is there to comment
without seeing their origins?

*

I want the Eastern section of our route to feel settled in, as if it is the most
natural thing in the world, to find a stupa or cairn high in Gleann an Eig, for
they fundamentally present different cultures saying the same thing.

*

We are imaging the landscape, perhaps trying to question the public
aversion to ritual, an uncertainty or awkwardness to be overcome, by taking
the mind out of itself through the act of walking and intensifying surrounding
phenomena. Strangely in Tibet there is no word for ritual, only the delineation
beween what activities a lay person and monk are allowed to participate in.

Out on the trek in Nepal in late winter, I have never encountered such a depth of silence. The high mountains have shrouded themselves in mist for the third day, so we have had only one tantalising view of silvery sunlight catching the vast flanks of a 7,000 metre peak soaring upwards in a gap between the clouds. One Sherpa guide, Chering, says as a Buddhist he is proud that the West is looking to his traditions for spiritual direction. Yet you can understand the Dalai Lama's plea for people to fully explore their own belief systems, before immersing themselves in cultural traditions born out of such a different perspective on life.

*

A climb up to Yangri Peak, setting off in darkness at 3am, moving steadily upwards through quiet woods. I place each of my steps into the crisp footprints of Ang Phurba, who is breaking trail, walking exactly on his line. At dawn, after five days of overcast skies, the first reveal of the Himalayas in perfect visibility. Nothing can prepare you for the sense of scale, the vastness and sheer number of peaks fading into the distance.

*

I had begun to realise, on a walk up Schiehallion, how slowly nature reveals herself to you. How it could take a lifetime to truly feel part of a particular landscape. The knowledge that leads to wisdom is hard come by. A real sense of knowing something, built out of experience and observation, seems to slip into place only when there is space for the thoughts to occur. Spending time in a special place is one of my keys, as it helps you to get beyond the limits of your background.

*

Fear could become a major factor, the threat or thrill of stepping into the unknown, also the ways of making tangible, less visible relations with the natural world. Actions like silvering water, drinking from a spring, placing a stone on a cairn, if they can be accepted as genuine affirmations on the ascent. If the work is to stand as more than just an interlinked series of installations, becoming a walked performance, an accumulation of knowledge, it will need to feel challenging without being life threatening. The forms given some

Yangri Peak, Nepal
Doug Scott

Opening and closing *pujas*,
Glen Lyon
Hilary Westlake

underlying symmetry by the flow of the illuminated route. Co-director Hilary Westlake notes that we will have to be careful of creating self-conscious participation. At best we will be creating doors between the visible and the invisible.

*

The journey is now set at two hours with the top dyke forming a symbolic barrier between our domesticated route and an un-meditated, inchoate region beyond – the otherworld. Glen Lyon was originally Gleann Fàsach – the empty or desolate glen. The general shift after the physical effort of the ascent is towards a more reflective atmosphere on the return leg. In attempting to understand other cultures can you gain a new perspective of your own?

*

A truly phenomenal night walk, the moon peeking out from behind clouds, throwing out strange shapes up and down the glen. The praying hands casting a solid black V shadow, framed ominously by the pyramidical form of Creag nan èildeag. It cannot be underestimated the extent to which weather will dictate the quality of the experience. On a cold, wet, windy night it will be about survival.

*

First press conference, I remembered out loud that I searched through over forty locations across Scotland over a two year period before finding Glen Lyon. That the work is as much about bringing forgotten things to the surface as creating something new. I also acknowledged the paradox of using technological and potentially intrusive means to 'enhance nature'. But *The Path* is set on a working farm, whose character has been affected by one thousand years of continuous human activity.

It is no wilderness.

*

An unbelievable evening hearing sounds and seeing our illuminations for the first time. It was so warm and still that a single blade of grass, when dropped, fell straight downwards. Recordings of the Nepalese singing bowls sounded spacious and immense, gently rolling off the hill. Ani Choying Drolma, the

Tibetan nun's voice swept and swirled across Sròn Eich, the mountain acting as a huge reverberation chamber. Climbing higher to the stupa cairn, built by the **nva** team and the recently arrived Sherpas, we saw an immense string of individual lights snaking back down a mile and a half to start. The joy of seeing that beautiful line, sensing the immensity of the work and what the team has achieved, after month upon month of battling to raise the finances and just convincing people to let it happen.

*

Overheard comms link on opening night:
'Roger, can you confirm if you are in the otherworld?'

'Nah DB, I'm just coming out of the fairy knolls'.

*

The opening night was still and quiet, the first paying audience spoke in whispers, a huge difference to the raucous social for local residents the previous night. The first walkers coming off the route looked so contented. The sense that we had got something right. Early stories – a photograph of a baby left in the butterlamp cave; three devout Christians refusing to walk sunwise round the stupa cairn and incredible feedback, an immediate sense that people were taking *The Path* on for themselves, a sense of ownership of the work that I hadn't anticipated.

*

Great moment, when neighbours in the glen start ringing to ask if they can take part as guides. Over the last two weeks, people have been standing outside their farms and cottages at night to marvel at the lights and listen to the sounds drift off the hill in the early hours.

*

Frighteningly positive reviews, am championed as the Thane of Glen Lyon in one, and am inevitably referred to as Inthane of Glen Lyon for the rest of the run. A tad melancholic, I wonder if we can ever create something on this level again. Maybe you just have one really good idea in a lifetime.

The Path
Alan McAteer

The Path
Alan McAteer

The Path
Alan McAteer

An opening fire *puja* on the hill led by Akong Rinpoche and the *sanga*, a closing ceremony by Lama Yeshe, fragrant juniper burnt as an offering. An introduction to all the **nva** team, on how Buddhism has adapted simple and effective systems of making land sacred, building on previous Bon-Po traditions. Ani Choying and Santa and Shree, the bowl players, cannot believe how at home they feel. Ang Phurba says that it is uncannily like the foothills of the Khumbu region.

*

Final day, and the work has proved to me that you can look for a practical, down-to-earth, spiritual side to life, with no notion of being sinful or fallen.

All that matters to me, by any faith's standards, is not to do harm to others. Through nature, without an intermediary, you can develop a direct way to find peace inside, get perspective, or just feel better about things. This is no system of belief, rather something that can become part of your daily existence. It's been a long haul this time for everyone who worked on *The Path*, but for most, the struggle has turned to fulfilment, especially with the depth of public reaction. Every up and down, wrong turn; and moment of insecurity has been worth it to reach this point.

*

I will never forget the last night. A mist dropped down to 1,000 feet and visibility was down to about ten paces, yet odd patches of clearness kept breaking out over the hill. The result was an unfolding drama of shifting scenes and atmosphere. Lights danced on the underside of gently dispersing clouds and could not even reach the firm surfaces of Sròn Eich. A huge bank of rolling fog absorbed them, which then emnated the strangest blue, dawn-like, effect. I walked the whole route for the last time, like I was walking in a dream, a softness permeating everything. How kind, after days of blustery rain, that we should be given this final gift. It is human nature to personalise the elements and you could not help but feel that on this night they were with us.

From Here to There

Doug Scott

The Storr recce
Angus Farquhar

At the dawn of this new century it is natural to look back to see what has been meaningful, to give purpose to the future. There are certain attitudes and traditions worth preserving to illuminate the way forward with confidence, to avoid stumbling, side-tracked into blind alleys.

There has been such an increase in the number of people taking up climbing, coupled with the growth of information technology, that inevitably there has been a rapid change in climbing values. As a result, climbing is going through a period of crisis. There is a danger that what was valuable may be lost, but there is also, as in any crisis, the opportunity to become more relevant, through bringing into sharp focus the reasons people took to climbing mountains in the first place.

There is, in humanity, an essential paradox. On the one hand we seek all ways and means to make our lives more comfortable, safe and certain; on the other, we know intuitively that only by taking risks and facing up to uncertainty are we going to stretch ourselves, go beyond ourselves, arrive at that moment of truth when we see deeper into the unknown.

Instincts for adventure, so deeply rooted over the past millennia as man evolved in the unpredictable, natural environment, now lie largely dormant. They are only given expression by chance or by artifice. The mountainside is a medium for adventure when the climber concentrates their attention, creates for themself heightened sensibilities and an awareness verging on the extraordinary, summoning up areas of their being which are normally hidden. These are times when a little light is let into our lives, and we remember those climbs so illuminated. So profound are these moments, even if they last only for a few seconds, that they are savoured with reverence. This is why every committed climber prefers to lead rather than follow. It is because these experiences are so profound that any diminution of the possibility of achieving them in the future causes consternation and even abhorrence amongst the regular mountaineering fraternity.

We came into this world, at heart, primitive tribal hunters with a set of basic instructions to be creative, exploratory, resourceful. We are designed to investigate, organise and create. It is a struggle to match our ancient, inherited qualities with the present situation of overcrowding. Will it all end up a human zoo, as Desmond Morris put it, like a 'hideously cramped animal menagerie of the last century or a magnificent human game park'?

Recently Greg Child, myself, and two Indian friends, Balwant Sandhu and Akhill Sapru, stumbled into the primary rain forest of Arunachal Pradesh. It was soon apparent that we were in an environment to which we did not belong. We would not have made the eighteen day journey through the jungle to the peaks on the Indo-Tibetan border without the help of the indigenous Nishi tribesmen. We would not have managed a week on our own. As it was, we suffered typhoid, malaria, blood poisoning, torn tendons and festering sores from leeches and dim dim flies, as well as a degree of despondency and helplessness not experienced on any other expedition.

Meanwhile, the Nishi, totally adapted to living on steep mountain sides covered in dense jungle washed by incessant rain, displayed all the attributes and energy of real mountaineers. They used, to ingenious effect, the jungle cane and creeper to bridge torrential side streams and the thunderous Khurung River.

Not having cattle to move, they preferred to take a direct line on the hillside, constructing ladders up rock steps rather than zig-zagging. They were physically very strong, with exceptional balance, moving over the most precarious terrain with grace and an economy of effort that allowed them to cover in a day, bare foot and laden, what would take incomers four or five without a load.

Throughout this ordeal they remained stoically indifferent to the horrendous and often dangerous conditions of travel, such as the way the slippery slope fell towards monster cliffs above the Khurung River in full flood. Not only were the Nishi kind and generous in taking good care of totally inept strangers, they were also warm and spontaneous, producing laughter and amusement at every opportunity. Time with the Nishi gives a snapshot of how presumably all our ancestors once were, for 200,000 years or so – a long time to have had the basic instinct of compassion for others. Dani tribespeople of New Guinea, and other remnants of hunter-gatherering nomadic peoples, give similar glimpses into our remote past. They are however a dying breed.

It seems to be a universally accepted factor amongst anthropologists that primitive uncivilised hunters are noteworthy for their 'good behaviour' until contact is made with 'civilised traders, government officials and the like'. It is hard to believe that man somehow contrives to be 'good' for his survival, more likely something happens in the process of living a simple hunter-gatherer existence that engenders feelings of respect for self and compassion for all.

In the process of climbing, in the Himalayas especially, the climber experiences extreme discomfort and uncertainty for long periods of time, and is at the limit of their endurance to such an extent that a change is inevitably affected in their state of being. It may be that, for a short time at least, there is a greater self confidence and consideration for others.

This state of being is likely to be more profound and longer lasting the more of their physical and psychological burden the climber is able to shed. The chances of achieving this are greater away from others, on a new route, in alpine style, with one or two friends, up a 6,000 metre peak, than in siege style on a popular route on a peak of 8,000 metres, where every move is reported to the expectant public back home. On the latter, the climbers are never committed to the climb, not only because they remain physically connected to the bottom by fixed ropes, but also because they never really leave home in the first place due to their media connections.

Most climbers move through the different climbing games until they find the one they can do best, or go back to the one that satisfied them the most. The ultimate climbs have to be those done in good style, on new ground, up into the so called 'death zone'. Now for those who have earned the right to be there, who go as friends supportive of each other in the spirit of co-operation rather than competition, with respect for the weather and place, prepared to await the moment when everything is right and everyone is in agreement as to when to go and where, the 'death zone' can be the place to climb beyond ego and self-importance. You come down more alive, and aware of all and everything like never before.

Evolution, it has been said, is the way back home to the primordial consciousness: it brings us full circle. Those going into the 'death zone', prepared to get off their backsides and be right there in the moment of being alive, taking the risk of stepping into the unknown, will have a better idea of this. (For those who have never been, this is all the way down at sea level in terms of gaining greater awareness of themselves). Cicero said in the first century 'that which has always fascinated man most is the unknown'. It is this facet of human nature that will keep climbing on course for another hundred years or more.

Designing with Nature

nva

The Storr: Unfolding Landscape is a journey of expanding horizons. It takes place in an area of such value, both culturally and ecologically, that its development over four years has been as much about how we make work, as why.

Previous work relied on huge oil burning generators towed into position by tractors, linking lights and control systems through many kilometres of heavy duty cables. *The Path*, **nva**'s major environmental animation in Glen Lyon, used enough power to light up a small village. While it looked stunning, the level of impact conflicted with the finer aspirations of the work. By contrast, *The Storr* has been set up without using a single generator and led to the team designing, prototyping and manufacturing a portable environmental lighting kit that has reduced power consumption and emissions by ninety percent.

This has been achieved by using rechargeable power sources, with radio controlled and programmable light systems adapted from the automobile and navigation industries. It points to a new way of operating in the natural landscape and has the potential to influence industry standards over the next twenty years, as the entire outdoor sector moves towards a more sustainable and thoughtful use of resources.

Production designers <slight> and environmental consultant Jo Hunt worked as part of the core **nva** team to explore every possible way to reduce the impact the work had on the Storr landscape. This involved the company raising significant additional finance to helicopter all heavy equipment into sensitive positions, rebuild the path network as a permanent legacy, and develop a monitoring procedure to ensure on a daily basis that footfall off the path was kept to a minimum. Any direct impact was then 'mitigated' by significant job creation, training and capacity building to support future schemes within the Trotternish community.

Despite the work being in situ for only seven weeks, it was treated as a permanent build under legislation at the time. This led to a three hundred page planning application which included a full Environmental Impact Survey, of the sort normally required by super quarries or wind farms. It was not an environment that invited attention and the design demanded almost continual revision and reassessment over four years. Imperiously indifferent to **nva**'s intentions, the ridge had 'spoken' many times over the period, finally dropping a mighty four thousand tonne rockfall onto the high path behind the Old Man of Storr in July 2004.

The entire area is protected by some of the most powerful conservation laws in Europe. How then to find the right way to match the rights of general access with the level of restraint needed to ensure that the site was left in better condition than on arrival? It is rare for temporary work to go through such stringent legal processes; planning and art rarely speak the same language.

The following extracts give an insight into some of the key issues which informed the design.

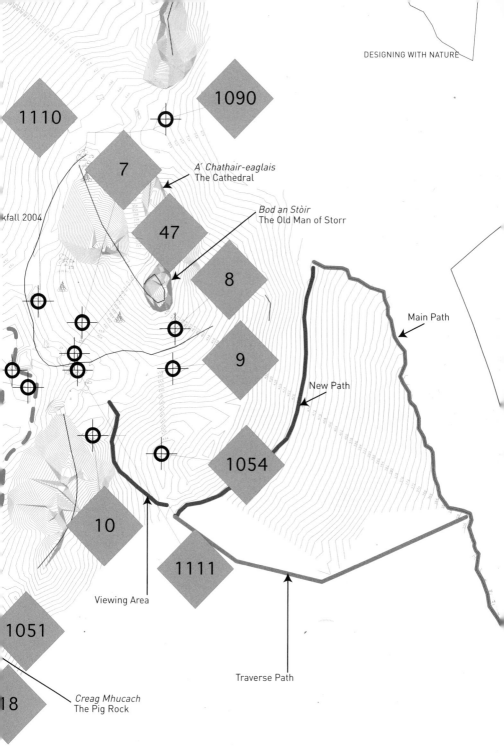

1110

1090

7

A' Chathair-eaglais
The Cathedral

47

Bod an Stòir
The Old Man of Storr

8

Main Path

9

New Path

1054

1111

10

Viewing Area

1051

Traverse Path

18

Creag Mhucach
The Pig Rock

xfall 2004

Issue: Site

The steep upper footpath had been seriously eroded and degraded through bad weather and over-use. No planning consent could be given without a total rebuild and an agreement to helicopter all heavy equipment, and hand-carry lighter equipment, directly into pre-defined locations.

Solution: Following the rockfall a commissioned investigation by the British Geological Survey revealed ongoing instability on the upper cliffs leading to a reassessment of the entire production methodology. This consolidated a move towards lighter equipment with lower power consumption, requiring a fraction of the cabling and infrastructure of a traditional outdoor event or festival. The danger area was avoided by creating a new permanent route in front of the Old Man of Storr. Original cabling would have required a twenty strong crew laying for five days; the new system required only two people over three days.

1 *Hansel and Gretel –*
The Brothers Grimm

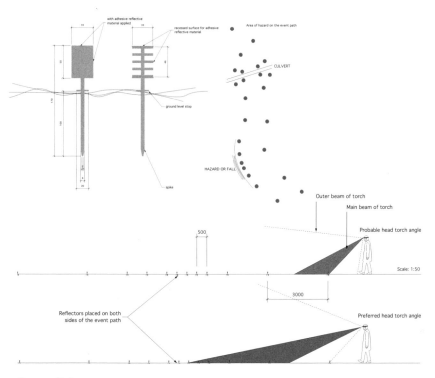

Issue: Safety

The route at night without illumination was potentially hazardous, particularly with the sudden shifts in weather that can be experienced on Skye.

Solution: A *Hansel and Gretel* navigation system using a lightweight Pezl headtorch, enabling each individual to illuminate their own route, combined with a way-finding system using an originally designed 'retro-reflective' marker. The light bounces back from each marker to the walker, clearly delineating the way ahead.

Gretel began to cry and to ask: 'How shall we ever get out of the wood?' But Hansel comforted her and said: 'Wait a little while, wait till the moon rises, and then we shall find our way.' When the moon rose... they began to walk back, guided by the pebbles, which glittered in the moonlight like newly coined silver money. They walked the whole rest of the night...[1]

Issue: Audience Impact

All impact in the most protected zones had to be contained within the path line. As Coire Faoin contains the rarest and most easily damaged plants on the entire ridge, any additional footfall in such an area was unacceptable.

Solution: Over three years more than five design solutions were developed for a viewing platform in Coire Faoin, varying from the use of recycled mobile phone masts to floating scaffolding structures and bench systems. It proved almost impossible to create a free standing structure without some additional staking or stability anchors. The final and simplest idea was to incorporate low 'thermarest' seats along the edge of the corrie path, which would then be made good at the end of the installation period, maintaining the lightest possible touch.

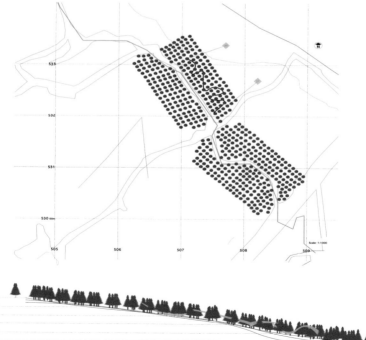

2003 Floating platform
Rolf Roscher

2005 Bench lines
<slight>

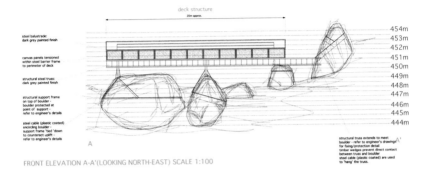

steel balustrade:
dark grey painted finish

canvas panels tensioned
within steel barrier frame
to perimeter of deck

structural steel truss:
dark grey painted finish

structural support frame
on top of boulder -
boulder protected at
point of support -
refer to engineer's details

steel cable (plastic coated)
encircling boulder -
support frame 'tied 'down
to counteract uplift -
refer to engineer's details

deck structure
20m approx.

454m
453m
452m
451m
450m
449m
448m
447m
446m
445m
444m

structural truss extends to meet
boulder - refer to engineer's drawings
for fixing/protection detail
timber wedges prevent direct contact
between truss and boulder
steel cable (plastic coated) are used
to 'hang' the truss.

A

FRONT ELEVATION A-A'(LOOKING NORTH-EAST) SCALE 1:100

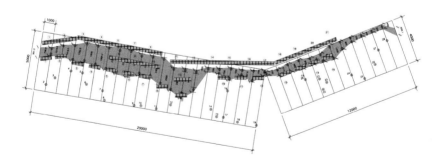

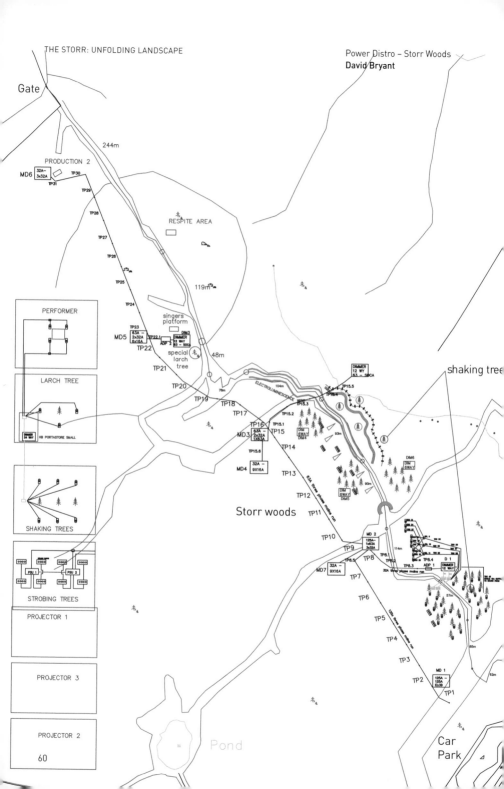

THE STORR: UNFOLDING LANDSCAPE

Power Distro – Storr Woods
David Bryant

Gate

244m

PRODUCTION 2

MD6 | 32A– 3x32A
TP30
TP31
TP29

TP28

TP27

TP26

TP25

TP24

RESPITE AREA

119m³

singers platform

MD5 | 63A– 2x32A 8x16A
TP23
TP22.1
DIM3
DIMMER 12 WY 63 – 30CA
ADP 1
TP22

special larch tree

TP21

48m

TP20

ELECTROLUMINESCENCE

78m

104m

DIMMER 12 WY 63 – 30CA

shaking tree

TP19

TP15.5

TP18

TP16.4

TP17

TP15.3

PERFORMER

TP16

TP15.2

TP15.1

MD3 | 63A– 2x32A 1X63A
TP15

LARCH TREE

DIM 6WAY DIM4

23m

HB PORTASTORE SMALL

TP15.6

DIM 24 WY

TP14

MD4 | 32A– 9X16A
TP13

DIM6 DIM 6WAY

DIM 6WAY DIM5

80m

SHAKING TREES

TP12

TP11

Storr woods

63A 3phase mains run

TP10

MD2 | 125A– 1x63A 3x32A

PSU 1   PSU 2

TP9

TP8

114m

TP8.4

STROBING TREES

MD7 | 32A– 9X16A
TP8.5

TP8

D 1

TP8.3

ADP 1

DIMMER 12 WY

PROJECTOR 1

32A 3phase mains run

TP7

TP6

TP5

125A 3phase mains run

TP4

TP3

PROJECTOR 3

TP2

MD 1 | 125A– ELCB

TP1

63m

PROJECTOR 2

60

Pond

Car Park

Issue: Renewable Energy

An aspiration to eliminate mains electricity completely was fulfilled by investigating renewable energy sources. Analysis revealed that sixteen 0.75m diameter wind turbines and over 60 square metres of solar panels would have given sufficient power to the generate the required capacity. The visual and ground impact of this system would have had a detrimental effect on the site.

Solution: Site tests, developed by <slight>, using mountain bike lights and marine technologies led the way to a recharging system, commissioned by David Bryant, that allowed twenty-two hours of stored energy to be expended over a nightly three hour period. The benefits of this system included the fact that any power input could be fed into it in the future: mains, solar or wind, as appropriate.

Issue: Environmental Monitoring

All footfall on site over the three month production period had to be evaluated, down to each individual movement of equipment, crew and audience, on a daily basis.

Solution: The number of access journeys to each lighting deck was calculated in advance of installation, based on the fragility of the ground. An Outdoor Event Management System, delivered through a bespoke database, was used to generate and monitor tasks, to log visitors and to track the environmental condition of the site throughout the build, event period and demount.

The knowledge accumulated, logged and stored during the design and implementation of *The Storr* leaves a valuable record of the methodology required for future interventions in sensitive natural locations.

Plants: Taking a slice through the Storr, from the 719m high summit to the sea 2km away, reveals its diverse range of geology and habitats.

Summit: bare, cold and wind blasted, the short mat grasses contain a unique mix of small hardy plants seen only on the highest mountain summits of the north west Highlands, and those usually seen growing low down in Iceland and the Faroe Islands.

Cerasticum articum, Arctic Mouse Ear

Cliffs: the hard basalt rock has been thrust up through old layers of seabed studded with fossils. As the ice sheet that covered most of Scotland 12,000 years ago melted, the side of the Storr slid down hill, opening up the Coire Faoin and revealing the cliffs.

Basalt rock columns and folded sediment layers

Crevices and the base of the cliffs: the cliff face is an inhospitable environment for plants, but where water runs down crevices, it slowly dissolves the lime rich basalt rock, thus creating a home for small arctic plants. Protected from the sun and from grazing sheep and rabbits, these plants have survived unchanged for thousands of years.

Minuartia sediodes, Mossy Cyphel and *Poa aplina,* Alpine Meadow Grass

Scree: below the cliffs, broken rocks form a wide band of rock scree, which provides a rich habitat for small ferns, long grasses and tiny plants called liverworts. These plants grow very slowly and are soft and easily damaged. The scree rocks protect them from disturbance.

Koenigia islandica, Iceland Purslane, *Botrychium lunaria,* Moonwort Fern, and *Harpalejeunarea molleri,* a liverwort with no common name

Boulders: the corrie is littered with large boulders that have fallen from the cliff; some thousands of years ago and others very recently. The surfaces of the old boulders are covered with a crunchy mat of overlapping lichens. As the surface dissolves in the rain it feeds ringed colonies of the minute plants. Some, the size of a 50p piece, are 300 years old. They are easily rubbed off the boulder surface. Some glow under UV light.

Pertusaria chiodectonoides and *Vestergranopsis elaenia,* two lichens with no common name

Moraine slopes: the short, sheep and rabbit grazed turf on the floor of the corrie and below the rock pinnacles is a complex lawn made up of grass and mosses, between which grow a collection of tiny liverworts, bryophytes and fungi. A half metre square of the turf can contain up to 80 different species of plants, which grow together. This grass habitat is unique and of international conservation importance.

Festuca ovina, Sheep's Fescue, *Alchemilla alpina,* Alpine Lady's Mantle, *Barbilophozia lycopodiodes,* a liverwort, *Geoglossum atropurpureum,* Darkpurple Earthtongue Fungus

Forest: the Storr woodland is an almost entirely man-made habitat. The site was deep ploughed with a bull-dozer, and spruce and pine trees were planted between 1970 and 1974. The trees have not been thinned and beneath them very little grows. The woodland does provide shelter for mammals and birds and is being opened up for more visitor access.

Norway Spruce, Sitka Spruce, Lodge Pole Pine

Peat bogs: the wet slopes above the road are covered with a deep layer of peat that has built up slowly over centuries. The dead plants do not decay in the cold and wet, and form sponge-like peat moss. The surface of the peat is acidic and wet: ideal conditions for heather, sedges, and midges.

Calluna vulgaris, Ling Heather and *Eriophorum vaginatum,* Hare's Tail Cotton Sedge

1 Use existing path for audience and staff access
2 Carry out servicing on decks, not standing on ground
3 Support rebuild of existing path to carry audience, staff and site visitors
4 No equipment on boulders and avoid boulders in all areas
5 Carry out work to reduce erosion rate and repair existing vegetation damage
6 No vehicles on site, equipment by helicopter, staff access on foot
7 Reduce and limit number of visits by staff to equipment and vary approach route
8 Move some cables every two weeks to avoid vegetation kill
9 Place equipment off ground on grid decks, with feet attachments
10 No fuels or chemicals on site, minimal galvanised equipment
11 No ground anchors
12 Choice of locations to avoid vulnerable areas at risk of erosion
13 Reduce stocking of grazing animals on site for duration of event
14 Choice of locations to avoid undisturbed and pristine areas
15 Change dates of event
16 Change line of helicopter access to reduce bird disturbance
17 Limit audience numbers and spread run of event
18 Use dark colours for all equipment
19 Place camouflage netting over production areas
20 Route cabling away from main path and radio controls for equipment
21 Erect warning signs on public roads and in local press and accommodation
22 Develop new path lighting/marking system that is unobtrusive by day
23 Choose locations that are hidden from path, where possible
24 Restrict light spill
25 Place corrie speakers close to main platform
26 Provide WCs on site, using waterless system
27 Control litter through briefing staff and audience, and providing bags with stewards
28 Survey of local accommodation providers to identify capacity and views
29 Sell tickets for highland games week to local residents and visitors only
30 Provide pre-event briefing, visit and information to local businesses and groups

31 Provide audience and staff with 'code of conduct' and induction briefing on site and at event
32 Run park and ride scheme for audience and allow no parking at site in evening
33 Provide audience with advance event information pack containing info on safety, fitness and service
34 Take audience in groups of c20 with a guide accompanying them at all times
35 Set up local information points in Staffin and Portree providing information and bookings
36 Install midge-eating machines at key locations and sell midge nets and repellent
37 Create a hospitality centre at Staffin community hall, designed and run by Staffin youth club
38 Work with local providers to put on a programme of daytime activities during the event run
39 Employ a local co-ordinator to recruit and support local staffing and local business suppliers
40 Provide project apprenticeship scheme for six school leavers, paired up with **nva** team members
41 Hold event launch in October 2004 to give advance notice to local people and national audience
42 Work with HC youth service to record and publish a compilation of the event experience
43 Target students from Skye in recruitment drive for seasonal staff
44 Provide training courses for local guides
45 Set up and run an event support and review group of local interests and representatives
46 Provide information through local press and radio on the lead-in and progress of the event
47 Use local specialists in arts, Gaelic culture, project administration and delivery
48 Set aside free event tickets for Gaelic speakers and learners from across Scotland
49 Maintain open access to site and car park during daytime
50 Use mains electricity via step down from overhead line across site
51 Schedule delivery of equipment to site to avoid peak traffic flows and avoid need for vehicles to wait on public road to unload
52 Provide crew transport by minibus to and from site, and have any staff visitors park at Production 1 only
53 Apply to HC for consent under Land Reform (Scotland) Act 2003, Section 11 for permission to restrict pubic access to the event area at night

54 Sell tickets in advance and off site, with no tickets available at entrance to site prior to show, to prevent queuing for last minute entry
55 Issue numbered identification for audience members to wear on site
56 Safety manager has power of veto over event performance if it does not meet safety standards or there are hazardous conditions on site
57 Environmental advisor has power of veto over event performance if it does not meet environmental standards or there is risk of damage to site
58 Install lights on trees to be used on descent of path by audience
59 Carry out trials of new event equipment during winter 2004: including cables, route markers, decks and other items
60 Move production area 1D to new and more discreet location.
61 No generators used on upper or lower sites
62 Construction period focused off-site
63 Use of additional helicopter lifts for get out
64 Use of fully integrated radio control system
65 Extended traffic control system put in place
66 Mountain rescue training for all guides
67 Live fire elements cut from production
68 Extension of community management beyond event period
69 Strip supplies of packaging and other waste material before taking on site and store waste in sealed bins
70 Carry out daily litter sweep of path and Storr Woods.
71 Sort all solid waste for recycling prior to disposal
72 Extend get out period to two full weeks
73 Enforce a no-smoking policy on-site at all times, to be observed by both staff and audience
74 Construct off-ground audience platform in Coire Faoin or alternative
75 Construct site entrance and interpretation area
76 Design new scatter light system that is portable, self-contained and self-powered
77 Erect additional road signs in consultation with HC roads
78 Station crew member in Coire Faoin during daytime to advise public visitors and reduce uncontrolled visits to equipment decks

Had this rock been on the plains of Hindostan instead of the mountains of Skye, it would have been an object of greater devotion than the Jaggernaut Pagoda.

J Macculloch, Geologist (1819)

The Old Man is a curious pillar in shape like an elongated pear, its base cut into, its head 150 feet above you. Sitting down below it and facing the precipices, you are struck at first with the weird desolation of the place. The ravine below is full of shattered rocks fallen from cliffs above; the hues of the rock, grey and black, are ghastly and repellent; an eerie wind sobs in its gullies; wisps of mist floating across its face give it an unearthly appearance, as its summit and bastions and shoulders loom out then disappear. Here is a scene for dark tragedies; here might lurk the fabulous creatures of the Celtic mythology; here might rise the altars of some horrid and ghastly faith propitiating the gloomy powers with human sacrifice.

J A MacCulloch, Anthropologist (1905)

Meditations in Landscapes

Neal Ascherson

1 Membership Newsletter
of the Islands Book Trust,
*Urras Leabhraichean nan
Eilean*, Port of Ness,
June 2005.

Landscapes are like the body of a parent, seen by a child. Some parts are
dear and familiar, like a smile, or the outstretched hands on which you know
so well the ring and the reddened finger-joints. But there are other parts of
a landscape which are strange and terrifying, as if glimpsed through the crack
of a bedroom door. We know we are not meant to see or visit these parts of
a father or mother, and yet we also know that they are parts of our innermost
world, parts of us.

Today I got the latest issue of the Islands Book Trust newsletter[1], and
there was something there which reminded me of such forbidden parts of
our own landscapes. Michael Robson was discussing Martin Martin's great
work (*A Description of the Western Islands*), written around 1695. He came
to a passage about South Uist, referring to a 'valley between two mountains…
called Glenslyte'. There was good grass there in summer. Martin tells us that
'the natives who farm it come thither with their cattle in the summer time,
and are possessed by a firm belief that this valley is haunted by spirits, who by
the inhabitants are called the great men; and that whatsoever man or woman
enters the valley without making first an entire resignation of themselves to
the conduct of the great men will infallibly grow mad…'

Who were these great men? The Gaelic popular culture of the islands (caught
as it faded by JF Campbell in 19th-century Islay) suggests that this was one of
many ways of referring to Fionn MacCumhail and his band of companions,
the Feinne. They were remembered in the oral myth-cycles as people who lived
in the landscape, and had sometimes even shaped it (hurling great stones to form
islands). But what did the heroes do in that enormous dream-geography which is
Ireland and western Scotland together? Above all they hunted, and feasted, and
hunted again. So there is this oddity: that a settled population, which had been
involved in subsistence agriculture on machair land and in alluvial soils
at the mouths of glacial glens for five thousand years, chose to understand its
landscape as a place not for planting (or even gathering) but for hunting deer.
And it was sung and told as an ecstatic pursuit, as if the one desire besides
battle among those 'great men', astride their magic horses or running through
the trees with their swords, was to be at the hunt of the Feinne. So there arose
one of the special genres of Gaelic poetry, an enamelled, visually brilliant verse
about hunters' landscapes; the hills, woods and plains used as scenery for the

2 From Duncan Ban MacIntyre's
   'Ben Dorain', in Iain Crichton
   Smith's translation.

rush of mounted heroes, of their dogs, of their beautiful quarry:

> *Herds with white rumps race –*
> *hunters in the chase. O I love the grace*
> *of these noble ones.*[2]

So 'big landscape', the higher places and most spectacular features, became
a sort of deserted stage on which superior beings had once performed.
The sight of certain peaks and glens brought their songs and stories to mind.
Occasionally (as in Glenslyte), they might still be encountered. But at the
same time a far more prosaic sense of 'small landscape' existed; the peasant's
love-hate of the soil and of every familiar stone in it, which at once provided
his family's life and wore out his own. 'If I were not born there and the very
dust of the place dear to me', said a crofter to the Taylor Commission in 1954,
'I would quit tomorrow'.

In the Romantic decades there arose appreciation of landscape 'for itself'.
Outlines, skylines and distant views were thought to impart moral feelings
(sublime or horrid, 'smiling' or 'frowning') through their own agency.
But that does not mean that people in pre-modern cultures were emotionally
indifferent to landscape. Archaeology now shows that human beings were
often sensitive to visual elements in landscape, and that Bronze Age cairns,
for instance, were frequently sited to be 'tombs with a view'. How often, in the
West, they occur on the crest of a raised beach, glacial terrace or alluvial mound
which opens out over long arms of the sea and distant mountains! Families of
cup-and-ring marks also have a clear relation to landscape, being cut almost
invariably on southward-facing sheets of rock, at a few hundred feet above
sea level and usually with a wide sight over water. Groups of early Bronze
Age ritual monuments (Kilmartin Glen, for example) may be laid out to
extend or emphasise the natural pattern formed by the ridges and glens
of local geology. What this sensitivity to landscape contained, we don't know.
Possibly it was to do with complex beliefs about creation or group origin,
which will never be accessible to us. But my own feeling is that those people,
between four and five thousand years ago, also responded to dramatic geological
patterning, and to the shock of sudden views, in ways which we can recognise.

'Cultural landscape' is the phrase currently in fashion among curators and heritage managers and the conservation industry. It's a good phrase, in the sense that it is holistic. It recognises that the Romantic appropriation of landscape as an instrument for solitary pleasure is inadequate. What we see out there is not just hill and field and wood, but a compound of changing geology and climate with a variety of human uses which have modified the 'natural' environment.

In a way, this is making landscapes 'democratic'. In Europe, and especially in crowded Britain, a phalanx of conservation bureaucracies has spread its control over almost all remaining 'wild' places, and many beautiful or scientifically fascinating places which are less than 'wild'. These may be wildlife charities (like the Royal Society for the Preservation of Birds) or woodland preservation charities or heritage quangos (historical or archaeological) or landscape trusts committed to preserving some stretch of coastline or upland moor in what is imagined to be its 'original' condition. All these bodies have shared two features: they are not accountable to local people (or in most cases to any electorate or community whatsoever), and the interests of human beings living in or around the places they control come second to the interests of corncrakes, 'native' oaks, sphagnum mires or 'historic integrity'. This strange extraction of human beings from the physical environment is nonsensical, even frightening. Its fallacy is epitomised in that notorious slogan advertising an environment whose bare hills, waterlogged glens and lack of population are the direct result of human agency: 'Visit the Highlands: Britain's Last Natural Wilderness'.

But this crass bureaucratic attempt to evict humanity from nature is now in decline. The 'cultural landscape' notion restores human beings to the ideas of place. A 'World Heritage Site' today may well include worked fields and houses, and scheduled landscapes are often selected for the traces of human activity they show. Scientific experts, including archaeologists, have had to climb down from their old assumption that only they have the right to interpret sites and decide how they shall be used. The new humility is well expressed in Rachel Butter's recent *Kilmartin: an Introduction and Guide*:

'This landscape has been valued in several opposing ways. The gravel terraces were attractive to people over 4,000 years ago; here they buried their dead and perhaps enacted the ceremonies which gave meaning to their lives. Recently the same terrace has been valued by some people as a source of gravel for building and a commercial resource, and by others as a source of information about how others lived in the past'.

Many Scots have for centuries grasped the 'cultural landscape' idea without knowing that they were doing so. Scotland, more than any other country, shows the mark of man wherever the eye turns. In part, this is because geology has dominated Scottish patterns of living, imposing an architecture of glacier-gouged valleys alternating with mountain ranges, which runs from north-east to south-west. In this architecture, human settlement and activity has been little more than a lichen which was able to get a grip in the less exposed crevices and surfaces of the land. Scotland has thin acid soil for the most part, and the rock, like a bone, pokes everywhere through the worn sleeve of turf or heather. Every mark made on its surface, every ancient path or new trench, leaves its scar on the skin. Scotland reveals not merely the unity of man and nature but – a much deeper revelation – the unity of life and non-life. To stare into this country from a high hill is to become aware that, at some level, bracken, rocks, man and sea are one.

Theologians have always preached that 'Man is made in God's image'. But I have yet to read or hear one who followed the logic of this assertion and admitted that God must look like Man. The same with landscape. It's become possible to see human beings as part of a natural environment, formed and given physical and social life by the water, crops and fish, by the hills and forests around them in childhood. But can the reverse – the thought of a landscape which is the image of human beings – have any sense to it?

I used to despise pseudo-archaeological brochures which claimed that the
hills around Glastonbury were enormous representations of the Zodiac signs.
Now, travelling across Argyll hills in the silence of ruined villages, I sometimes
fear there is a big life and a voice under those hills. The poet David Jones
wrote this:

> Are the slumbering valleys
> him in slumber
> are the still undulations
> the still limbs of him sleeping?
>
> Is the configuration of the land
> the furrowed body of the lord
>
> Are the scarred ridges
> his dented greaves
>
> Do the trickling gullies
> yet drain his hog-wounds?
>
> Does the land wait the sleeping lord
> or is the wasted land
>
> That very lord who sleeps?

The Via Negativa

Robert Macfarlane

Night brings great strangeness to a landscape. Samuel Taylor Coleridge once compared walking the Lake District at night to a newly blind man feeling the face of a beloved child: the same care of attention, the same deduction by form and shape, the same familiar unfamiliarity. His analogy is only half right. For to walk at night is not fully to enter the province of the blind. At night one is always assured of a sunrise, however mist-obscured or cloud-hung. Some day will come – this the night-walker knows. But the strangeness of night, the way it obliges us to see and to feel and to hear differently: this is unmistakably true, and well attested to by artists and by visionaries.

One thinks, for instance, of the French pilot and writer Antoine Saint-Exupéry, who in the 1920s made pioneering flights over the Sahara and the Mediterranean, and who travelled for hours over utterly lightless landscapes and seascapes. Night for him should have been an enemy, another antagonist in his already dangerous aerial world. But in his books – the greatest works of all aerology – Saint-Exupéry writes adoringly and repeatedly of night, and how darkness 'urges one to discover a new meaning in familiar objects of vision'. 'God, how empty this planet is', he exclaimed exultantly after one long night-flight, 'the rivers and the shady woods and the habitations of men seem to exist through conjunctions of happy chance! There is so much rock and sand and darkness!'

Or one recalls the great mountaineer-writer WH Murray, who so loved night-walking in winter mountains. Murray once said – sung, perhaps, is a verb which better carries the hint of the psalmic in Murray's declaration – that 'the hardships of night-climbing are far outweighed by the joys of dwelling for a space on snow-fields close to the sky, where the dawn and sunset come like armadas in slow and solemn grace, and the very air has a beauty, which we call purity.'

Or one thinks of James McNeill Whistler, and his extraordinary series of London mood paintings from the 1870s, the *Nocturnes*. A contemporary of Whistler's, speaking of the chalk drawings on brown paper that the artist made in preparation for painting the *Nocturnes*, observed that they were 'drawn in the dark, by feeling not by sight'. For certain of his canvases, Whistler arranged to be rowed to the centre of the Thames in the middle of the night. From the row-boat, he would sit and stare for hours at the ghostly shapes of warehouses and factories on the South Bank – and he would then go back at dawn and paint them. This was how Whistler made the Thames – that most familiar, most represented of rivers – strange again. He brought the dark to bear on it.

Night is visionary, and night in the mountains doubly so. For mountains have always been places to which we have travelled in pursuit of the sight of the seer. In its simplest form, this is because of the rare optical powers which altitude affords the human eye. Mountains, hills and high ground offer places from which your eye can traverse pleasingly between different orders of life: where events, objects and existences which are normally dispersed in space and time can be experienced simultaneously, and at a single glance. Altitude – with good weather – makes possible the panorama: the Greek word for 'all-sight' or 'all-embracing view.' 'From an Alpine mountaintop', wrote the Swiss naturalist Conrad Gesner in 1541, 'one might observe on a single day the four seasons of the year.' The great seventeenth-century French traveller, Maximilien Misson, noted that from the rough stone balconies of the Chartreuse St Martin, perched high above Naples, a spectator could survey the outline of the city itself – its harbour, breakwater, lighthouse and castles – then move southwards, over the scalloped coastline with its white rocks, and then northwards, to the black bulk of Vesuvius, with thick lines of smoke coiling upwards like fakirs' ropes out of its crater.

But of course at night, these views, these new orders of connection, are not available to the mountain-traveller. Instead, other types of vision assert themselves: sonic, olfactory, tactile, memorious. The sensorium is transformed. Recollections and associations swarm out of the darkness, like sounds. One becomes even more aware of landscape as a medley of effects, a mingling of geology, memory, nature, movement. The landforms are still there, but they exist as presences: inferred, less substantial, but more powerful for it. One is aware of an island's coast, near at hand but out of sight; of the relentless dark momentum of the ocean; of a storm moving over distant landmass, with blue filaments of lightning linking sky and earth; of rock towers weighing millions of tons balanced above the traveller in the darkness.

Night, then, is not a blinding of sight, but its rerouting. Nor is sight itself abolished. Even on moonless nights, the perceptive capacity of the eye is formidable. In 2002, through ancient woodland in the Leconfield Estate in West Sussex, the land artist Andy Goldsworthy laid out a mile-long trail made of pulverized chalk mined from the Sussex Downs. Arriving at the path after sunset, one followed the shining path alone, beneath dense canopies of birch and oak, and through open glades. The chalk collected and returned what light there was with enormous efficiency. When the moon was full, it shone like phosphorous. On overcast nights, it glowed with a strength sufficient to illuminate the white bark of the birches which lined it – as though one were moving through a shallow luminous valley. The forest – a fairy tale world – came weirdly alive in this new light.

At night, in a mountain landscape such as that of Skye, one moves not through the realm of fairy tale, but into the realm of psycho-geology. One becomes aware that one is walking through the depths of time, as well as through physical space. The layers of imagined history, both human and geological, are as real as the rock and grass beneath one's feet. The imagination curls around the landscape, sensing its shapes, and intuiting the forces which have brought it into being: ice, fire and water. John Ruskin, who liked to walk by night, was superbly aware of these forces. If you have read Ruskin on mountain scenery, you will know that before his gaze, the landscape yielded up the stories of its making. Meditating on the nature of granite, with its mix of minerals and colours, Ruskin dreamt of the violence inherent in its creation: 'The several atoms have all different shapes, characters, and offices; but are inseparably united by some fiery, or baptismal process which has purified them all'. Basalt – another Skye stone – he perceived to have at one stage in its career possessed 'the liquefying power and expansive force of subterranean fire'. Seen through the optic of Ruskin's prose, geology becomes war; the view from the Storr, say, becomes a panorama over battlegrounds upon which competing armies of rock, stone and ice have fought for epochs, with incredible slowness and unimaginable force. To read Ruskin on rocks was, and still is, to be reminded of the earth's furious energies; those same energies which surge around one with especial force at night.

Mountains, and the wild landscapes out of which they rise, seem to answer an increasing imaginative need in us. More and more people are discovering a desire for them, and a powerful solace in them. At heart, mountains, like all wildernesses, challenge our complacent conviction – so easy to lapse into – that the world has been made for humans by humans. This becomes only truer at night. Most of us exist for most of the time in worlds which are humanly arranged, themed, and controlled. One forgets that there are environments which do not respond to the flick of a switch or the twist of a dial, and which have their own rhythms and orders of existence. Mountains correct this amnesia.

By speaking of greater forces than we can possibly invoke, and by confronting us with greater spans of time than we can possibly envisage, mountains dispute our excessive trust in the man-made. They pose profound questions about our durability and the importance of our schemes. They induce, I suppose, a modesty in us.

Mountains also reshape our understandings of ourselves, of our own interior landscapes. The remoteness of the mountain world – its harshnesses and its beauty – provides us with a valuable perspective on to the most familiar and most charted regions of our lives. It can subtly reorient us, and readjust the points from which we take our bearings. In their vastness and in their intricacy, mountains stretch out the individual mind and compress it simultaneously: they make it aware of its own immeasurable acreage and reach and, at the same time, of its own smallness.

Most importantly, mountains quicken our sense of wonder. The true blessing of mountains is not that they provide a challenge or a contest, something to be overcome and dominated (although this is how many people have approached them). It is that they offer something gentler, and infinitely more powerful: they make us ready to credit marvels – whether it is the dark swirls which water makes beneath a plate of ice, or the feel of the soft pelts of moss which form on the lee sides of boulders and trees. Being in the mountains, by night as by day, re-ignites our astonishment at the simplest transactions of the physical world: a snowflake a millionth of an ounce in weight falling onto one's outstretched palm; water patiently carving a runnel in a face of Jurassic clay; the apparently motiveless shift of a stone in a scree-filled gully. To put a hand down as you climb up towards the Old Man of Storr, and to feel the ridges and scores in a rock where a glacier has passed; to hear how the Trotternish hillside comes alive with moving water after a rain-shower; to see moonlight filling

Certain parts of this essay are reproduced from *Mountains of the Mind* with kind permission of Granta

miles of Atlantic coastline like an inexhaustible silver liquid – none of these is a trivial experience.

Mystic theology speaks of the idea of the *Via Negativa*. It means the Dark Road, or the Way of Darkness. According to the doctrine of the *via negativa*, no predicates attach to God; no words may legitimately be used to describe Him. He is 'not this, not that'. But in stripping from the perceiver's mind its delusions about God, and in eliminating all that is not God, the acceptance of the *via negativa* helps the individual to move towards the heart of the divine mystery. One need not be a mystic, or a believer of any kind, to sense that night – the Way of Darkness – brings one closer to that which is ineffable in a landscape.

The Black Wood

David Greig

You would think the woods would be dead in winter but a few mushrooms survive the frosts. On stumps and fallen branches you can find the cartilaginous pink cups of Judas Ear. Sometimes you find white Angels Wings as late in the year as December. Wood Blewits make the best eating though: pale lilac toadstools with a brown patch on top like a caramelised skin. I found hundreds down by the dam. A fairy ring of them surrounding a stand of pines. I didn't know they grew in fairy rings. Later I'll cook them up with bacon and cream. You would think the woods would be dead but there's always something to be found.

The snow has been falling for an hour or so now and we stop and sit down on a heather bank. I take out a hot flask of honey, lemon and whisky. The cup steams in the cold air. Our breath comes in clouds. I'm glad we came down to the Black Wood again. Back up at the house, on the moor, the wind would be pulling at us and cutting our faces but here, amongst the ancient pines, there's barely a breeze. And it's quiet. The fat flakes of snow fall down slowly, silently to settle.

I suppose we should talk, sort things out, but even as words start to form in my mind they suddenly seem so heavy and the attempted sentences so entangled that I can't quite be bothered to speak them. I lie back on the bank. The heather and snow make a soft mattress. I close my eyes and listen to the wood. The pines creak. Branch clatters against branch in the high canopy. Her waterproofs rustle as she sips the hot toddy. High and far away I can hear a plane, or maybe it's a car somewhere on the other side of the loch. I hear my own breathing. I hear my own heartbeat. It's quiet here but it's not silent. I've been in amongst a Sitka Spruce plantation. In there, in that all day long darkness where even the birds are hushed, you can find a real silence – a world empty of sound, heavy and dead.

Earlier in the year I took my kids for a walk up a wee hill. The way down took us along a forest track through some old plantation forest. I say 'old', I just mean this crop was planted before the forestry commission brought in the new aesthetic rules that soften the edges of forest with a few broadleaved trees. The track wound snakewise downwards through the close planted trees as though between two tall, dark, wooden pallisades. The day was coming to an end and, for a joke, the kids and I took what we thought was a short cut through the woods. They wanted to jump out onto the path a little way ahead and surprise their mother who was walking behind us. We held hands and plunged into the plantation.

Plantation monocultures bear the same relation to native forest that a field of wheat bears to a wild meadow, or an intensive piggery to a herd of wild boar. The plantation is – in essence – industrial woodland. Even as we were only metres in I was being attacked by sharp branches at eye level. The kids were getting scratched and their clothes caught. The floor beneath us was uniform needle brown. I thought it would be a matter of moments before we emerged onto the path again but, in avoiding the stabs and scrapes of the trees, we'd wandered off course and now we were deep in the wood. We hit a patch of clear felling – an apocalyptic landscape of twisted stumps and thick swampy mud. The children were becoming agitated. They knew we were lost. I knew that we only had to keep heading east and we would – eventually – hit open land. I also knew that, depending on where we were, that could mean struggling on for two minutes or two hours through this landscape of thick woody darkness and bog.

My daughter never liked woods – even as a baby. Here in the plantation she had held her nerve against the panic for some twenty minutes but I could tell she was about to crack. As an adult, I could rationalise that this landscape was simply a product of human agriculture and that it contained no objective danger. To her, a seven year old, and to her five year old brother, they had quite simply wandered into the landscape of their nightmares. Just then we stumbled across a cache of animal bones. A fox, probably, had dragged the corpse of a lamb, probably, deep into the wood. A little further on – more bones – this time the skull of a deer. Even I began to wonder what hellish creature kept this gruesome ossuary. Moments later we emerged back on to the path and into the bright afternoon sunlight.

Later that summer we spent an afternoon in the Black Wood picking chanterelles. We moved together slowly as a family. We wandered off the path, our gaze combing the bracken floor looking for treasures. The children roamed off like outriders, climbing trees, hiding amongst the undergrowth, bringing things back to us to identify. As we wandered we grazed on blueberries and wood sorrel. We were all spread out as we moved through the wood, sometimes out of sight but always within earshot of each other. When we finally got back to the car, the baskets heaving with food, I realised we must have spent seven hours wandering in the wood and, during all that time, the children had needed almost no attention from us. I was reminded of an archaeologist who, describing life in a prehistoric forest settlement, said 'for Neolithic children, the line between foraging for food, and play, was a very thin one.'

It's now January and I'm lying in the snow trying to work out where I am in my life. Listening to the wood I can feel my own mind quieting. I have the sense of bathing in cool stillness. I open my eyes. I see the snowflakes fall towards me out of the dark sillhouetted lattice of the pine canopy. The falling flakes create the illusion that I am moving steadily upwards through a world of fat white stars.

This idea of woodland as a source of healing, a place of reflection, and a sustainer of life has been almost entirely lost in this country. It survives only in fragments. Our native pinewoods are almost all gone. The Black Wood is only a few square kilometres in size. There's a larger patch up near Rothiemurchus and a small area at Achallader – you can see it from the train on the West Highland line between Tyndrum and Rannoch Station. But apart from that, the Caledonian Pine Forest has mostly gone. What we call 'forest' now, what our children experience as woodland, is – in most instances in the Highlands – a forest track through a crop of Sitka. You even find the local authorities packaging these experiences as 'forest park', as though a walk through an abbatoir might be described as a safari.

Sorley MacLean, writing of the Raasay woods of his childhood, describes the forest as 'a high green room' and supporting its roof: 'the pillars of the room, the noble restless pines.' Whenever I am in the Black Wood, whichever season it might be, I always feel that I am entering a religious interior every bit as intricately constructed, as ornate and as sacred as any gothic cathedral. Kathleen Jamie, thinking of poetry, describes 'noticing' as a form of prayer. Perhaps this is why I am drawn back to the Black Wood season after season. Perhaps this is why I find in it healing. Perhaps this is why it stills me into quietude. The woods are a place of endless noticing.

Paths of our Ancestors

John Purser

When you climb up to the so-called Old Man of Storr, you are not just on a journey into the wilds of nature, but a journey along paths taken by many herdsmen and women before you, and by their cattle.

Celtic culture is deeply rooted in cattle management, and keeping cattle in the Highlands is not like keeping cattle on a farm. Here they are not only a part of the landscape, but the bearers of knowledge of that landscape – a knowledge which, if we are attentive, we can in part acquire from them.

On the crofts and in the high places, they know all the different qualities of the grass and trees, of shelter from wind and rain depending upon their direction, and of where a breeze can be found on midgey days. They will go down to the sea to eat seaweed if they are hungry for salt and minerals. They also know where they want to give birth. Some prefer privacy and concealment in the woods where they may even hide the calf under dead bracken. Others will give birth in the open with the rest of our little neighbourly herd watching. On one occasion, the mother's calf of the previous year was so excited he rushed down the hill before the others to give his new half-sister a welcome sniff and lick. This is their territory more than ours and, if they can smell sexual potential on a neighbouring croft, fences are not to be relied upon unless they are in the very best of condition.

Each May the cattle are driven out onto the moors, cows and calves together, for the calves get to drink all their mothers' milk. And each September they are brought back in to the crofts. They know where they are going, and a lead cow will usually decide the route across the bog lands and rock, to the places where streams can be crossed or cliffy bits negotiated, remembering them from previous years and from her predecessors, and exemplars from hundreds of generations of cattle on these lands; for these paths are not just decades or centuries old, many of them have been around for millennia – yet most visitors will not even notice their presence.

It is not only these ancient ways of the cattle that are relevant to the landscape, but also their voices. Amongst the most moving sounds you can hear are those of a cow calling a very young calf to her side – *tarruingeach* is the word in Gaelic to describe it. It is the gentlest of sounds, appealing and attracting irresistibly. Equally lovely can be the sound of cattle calling to each other over distances and across water. Though they may be divided by hundreds of fences and many roads, and cannot see each other, in the quiet of the evening when cars and motor boats have gone to bed and mankind has gone to its televisions, they call out across ten or more miles, perhaps even recognising each other's voices.

Do not think of these beasts as dumb, and do not imagine that their voices are mere tools of Darwinian necessity. They feel and they express their feelings – especially the poor bull calves when being castrated! Their silence can also be eloquent. A mother will stand by her dead calf, though the eyes have already been eaten out of it, and there will be no calling from her; the next day you might find she has moved away a little but has not joined the rest of the herd; but with her will be her calf of a previous year, mother and son together, sharing their distress.

These kinds of relationship are rarely observed in cattle nowadays because their families are broken up almost immediately, but in the past, and in a few places today, the intimate relationship between families of cattle and families of humans was of vital significance. One of the most famous of *pìobaireachd* – an extended piece of pipe music – is the *pìobaireachd Maol Donn*, also known as *MacCrimmon's Sweetheart*. It is a lament for the death of a favourite cow – and it is a favourite among pipers today, centuries after it was composed. The fact that a major piece of music was composed in memory of a family cow underlines the depth of the connection between people and cattle in Gaelic tradition and, specifically, in the music of our national instrument.

But there were much older instruments belonging to the peoples who herded cattle in Ireland and Scotland – the beautiful curved bronze horns from the Bronze Age itself, of which many still survive. The originals – some still playable – are derived in form from the horns of cattle and can reproduce the sounds of cattle, amongst other things. They date from three millennia ago and, with their accompanying rattles shaped like a bull's scrotum, they carry with them a fertile memory of a great herding culture. Two of the most central Celtic myths are the *Táin Bó Cúalnge* and the *Táin Bó Fraích* and they are about cattle, with the outcome of the first decided by a battle between two bulls. Fertility is, of course, the single most important aspect of cattle rearing. A bull firing blanks produces no calves. A milking cow without a calf eventually goes dry.

The Old Man of Storr is not unrelated to such realities, for it is not the *bodach* or 'old man' at all: it is a *bod* in Gaelic – a penis – and in my book it is as likely to be that of a bull as a human.

Besides being able to imitate the sounds of cattle, bronze horns can also convey a sense of fear or of magic – sounds which relate to the mythology of the cattle, into which much that is magical is woven. That deeper sound world which is shared by all living things, in which the sounds of warning, of enticement and allure, have some strange commonality beyond analysis, will carry to you the sounds of our ancestors, human and animal, from deep in their throats. Listen in the silence and you too may, in imagination, follow those paths where human and animal, reality and myth, meet without embarrassment in natural companionship.

Geology of
the Storr

Chris Tyler

The Earth probably formed from a swirling mass of gas around the young Sun about 4,400 million years ago. For millions of years it was a molten mass, constantly bombarded by asteroids and great chunks of rock… as it finally cooled, water could condense, and rained down, eventually forming the ocean.

Heat from the molten core of the earth, caused by radioactivity, induces convection currents in the mantle, which makes the crust of the earth split apart; this leads to continental drift. For unimaginable aeons, continents have split apart, drifted across the planet, and collided and joined again… oceans have opened up, and closed again… as continents collide they form great mountain chains, as high as today's Himalayas, which are worn down by the forces of erosion, leaving just the rocks from the roots of the mountains, highly metamorphosed, altered by immense heat and pressure… this process has occurred again and again over hundreds of millions of years; continents have split apart, sailed across the globe and rejoined into 'supercontinents', then split once more.

Most recently (about 360–430 million years ago) an ancient ocean, Iapetus, disappeared as two continents collided to form Pangaea; the resulting mountain chain, the 'Caledonian Orogeny', was eroded away over time.

Our story starts in the Jurassic period, around 200 million years ago, when Skye was part of a shallow marine shelf. The warm seas teemed with life, and the muds and sands laid down formed sedimentary rocks full of fossils. Those of ammonites and belemnites (molluscan relatives of today's Nautilus) are common, especially along the shore at Bearreraig Bay, below the Storr Loch's dam. Ammonites were spiral shelled, belemnites were straight; both would have been like an octopus or squid with a shell. Dinosaur footprints can be seen at Staffin, and dinosaur and ichthyosaur bones have been found. Great beds of fossilised oyster-like shells occur along the east Trotternish shore.

Much later, around 65 million years ago, the Earth's crust was starting to split apart as the supercontinent Pangaea broke up, and Greenland began to split away from north-western Europe to form the Atlantic Ocean. Extensive systems of fractures developed, through which vast amounts of magma welled up and erupted. This formed very liquid lava, rather like that found today in eruptions on Iceland, and over a million years or so built up the vast lava plateau of northern Skye. (The line of huge volcanoes of Skye, St Kilda, Rum, Ardnamurchan, Mull, and Antrim form a sort of initial, failed attempt to split apart and start the Atlantic ocean opening up. The eventual split occurred further west, at Rockall.) The individual lava flows can be clearly seen in the cliffs of the Storr, some up to 25 metres thick.

Each eruption must have been a devastating event, probably destroying forests and wildlife over large areas. Between eruptions there could be quiet periods of thousands of years, as shown by layers of sedimentary rocks which accumulated between lava layers, as river systems and lakes developed, and life returned and flourished on the rich volcanic soils. The tops of some flows were weathered into the red soils typical of today's tropics; such soils can still be seen in places in the cliffs of Trotternish.

The accumulation of lava ended up several hundred metres thick, and is responsible for the stepped or 'trap' landscape of north and west Skye, with its flat-topped hills.

Some of the lava did not make it to the surface, but was injected between layers of the older, sedimentary rock, cooling rather more slowly and forming 'sills' of a hard rock called dolomite. A thick sill of dolomite underlies the Storr.

The huge, mile-high volcano which produced all this lava has long since been removed by erosion; the Black Cuillins are the solidified remains of the magma chambers beneath it, composed largely of gabbros (which cooled very slowly deep underground and hence had time to form large crystals, giving them their celebrated roughness, which makes them great for climbing. Basalt is of similar composition but cooled quickly, forming small crystals and therefore smoother rock, which can be very slippery when wet).

During the height of the last glaciation, about 21,000 years ago, Skye was covered by the great ice sheet flowing from the Scottish mainland. Ice up to 1,000 metres thick flowed down from the mountains, scouring and deepening the troughs that would form Loch Alsh, the Inner Sound and the Sound of Raasay. The ice sheet crossed Trotternish heading north-west, and only a few hilltops stuck out of the ice as 'nunataks'… including the Storr, Beinn Edra and Meall na Suiramach. The ice sheet melted around 14,000 years ago, leaving a landscape covered with an undulating sheet of gravelly debris or 'till'.

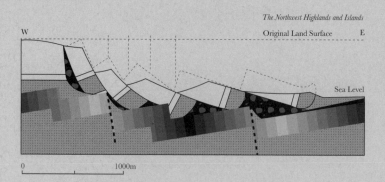

The Northwest Highlands and Islands

W — Original Land Surface — E

Sea Level

0 ————— 1000m

There was a final short glaciation from 12,500 to 11,500 years ago, when a small valley glacier formed in Coire Scamadal, on the north of the Storr. During this time Skye and the surrounding area would have been rather like today's Arctic Tundra.

The evidence of glaciation is everywhere in Skye, from the 'hummocky drift' at Sligachan (the multitude of small hillocks, called *Cnocan an Sìth* or Fairy Hills in olden days) to the U-shaped valleys of Glen Drynoch and Glenbrittle. As a glacier flows along it tends to deepen and steepen existing valleys by the abrasive action of the rocks and stones it carries within it. This was happening beneath the ice sheet grinding its way through the Sound of Raasay, so when the ice all finally melted it left huge steep cliffs along the Trotternish escarpment, with the great thickness of basalt lavas resting on relatively weak sedimentary Jurassic rocks. These inevitably gave way, leading to some of the biggest landslides in Britain. As the huge weight of ice was removed from the land, earthquakes would have occurred as the earth re-adjusted, and this may have caused some of the landslides. The result was a series of enormous chunks of basalt peeling off the cliff and starting their slow slide downhill, eroding as they went into fantastic spires and pinnacles, as seen at the Quiraing and the Storr.

This process must have been going on for many thousands of years, as many landslide blocks further down the hill have been smoothed by the passage of ice and capped by glacial till. The largest and most rugged pinnacles, like the Old Man of Storr, must have peeled off the cliff within the last 14,000 years, and are still moving slowly downhill, very quickly in geological terms, but imperceptibly to us. In a few hundred years the Old Man and his companions will have slid further and eroded away to be replaced by new blocks, in what is a highly dynamic and ever-changing landscape.

Skye & Raasay as Symbol

(in the poetry of Sorley MacLean)

Meg Bateman

Craobh nan Teud
'The Tree of Strings'

Sorley MacLean's poetry concerns itself with the starkest of questions about self-worth and the nature of time. It would be painfully abstract if it was not for his use of landscape as symbol. It is the landscape that gives form and sensuousness to his ideas and that lets him communicate them as emotion. He circles between the abstract and the specific. He is at once himself and everyman. Skye is recognisably itself and a terrible roller-coaster of self-loathing, exhilaration, tenderness and despair. Reading his poetry can feel like a physical work-out. To separate MacLean's art from the landscape would be to separate form and content.

His poetry is rarely easy and never cosy. He wrestles with himself, not in the shelter of the indoors with the distraction of other people, but in the most exposed and elemental settings, on the bare rock of the Cuillin, by the ocean, or below the stars. They represent the lonesomeness of the individual, the blankness of life and the perspective of eternity. The stars are cold and indifferent, for MacLean felt the presence of no benign God; it is ourselves who must rise from the morass of our compromised existence and make some worthwhile mark. The landscape is also a landscape of the mind. It is both majestic and broken, where his poems run like mad wolves in pursuit of beauty and where art, 'a flower to windward', grows on the bare rock.

Air cruas nan creag	On the hardness of rocks
tha eagar smuaine,	is the ordered thought,
air lom nam beann	on the bareness of mountains
tha 'n rann gun chluaine;	is the forthright verse,
air mullach beò	on a living summit
tha treòir nam buadhan,	is the might of talents,
air àirde ghil	on a white summit
tha 'n lios gun luaidh air.	the garden that is not named.

An Uair a Labhras Mi Mu Aodann'
'When I Speak of the Face'

Sometimes a direct vector may be drawn between symbol and symbolised. There is an elegance to *'Am Mùr Gorm'*/'The Blue Rampart', in the equivalents made between the stretching sands of Talisker and the poet's expectations, between the uneven moors and his reason, between the moods of the sea and his own moods. The symbolism is also simple in the poem *'An Uair a Labhras Mi Mu Aodann'*/'When I Speak of the Face'. The poet's vantage point on the top of the Cuillin, from where he surveys the oblique sunlight on the bogs, parallels the heightened awareness he has of human achievement and suffering through the experience of love.

Ach chunnaic mi bho àird a' Chuilitheann	But I have seen from the height of the Cuillin
gathadh glòir is breòiteachd duilghe;	darting glory and the weakness of sorrow;
chunnaic mi òradh lainnir grèine	I have seen the gilding light of the sun
agus bogach dhubh na brèine;	and the black rotting fen;
's eòl dhomh seirbheachd gheur an spioraid	I know the sharp bitterness of the spirit
nas fheàrr na aoibhneas luath a' chridhe.	better than the swift joy of the heart.

More often MacLean's symbolism is not so straightforward. The questions his poetry poses have no answers, only further questions. How are we to live? How can we know wholeness? What lasts of human endeavour? This dialectic accounts for MacLean's symbolism shifting, for meanings which change even within a verse, for symbols which simultaneously represent the seeker and the sought.

At the simplest level, *'Coilltean Ratharsair'*/'The Woods of Raasay' is about growing up. Firstly, the child is contained by the woods which clothe his imagination and with which he unconsciously shares a life force. Life is joyful, musical, exuberant, as is the metre of the poem.

Ùrlar frainich is beithe
air an t-seòmar àrd uaine,
am mullach 's an t-ùrlar
trom dhathte le suaimhneas:
mith-chuachan na sòbhraig,
bileag bhuidhe air uaine;
is cuilbh dhìrich an t-seòmair,
giuthas òirdhearc an luasgain.

Floor of bracken and birch
in the high green room;
the roof and the floor
heavily coloured, serene:
tiny cups of the primrose,
yellow petal on green,
and the straight pillars of the room,
the noble, restless pines.

After the carefree security afforded by the woods, the demands of the intellect appear as the Cuillin seen through the trees. The Cuillin is both a fire-dragon and a beautiful white unicorn, reflecting the double-edged sword of the intellect which brings both understanding and dissatisfaction. Likewise the moon and stars appear and the poet is exercised 'to work out their genesis'. Sexuality appears as a face in the wood and as a snake, the thrust of pain in the love-making connected to the thrust of the Cuillin, the male principle penetrating the female principle, the intellect penetrating the unconscious. The poet envies the woods their unconscious, untaught existence; man, by contrast, maimed by consciousness, loses his innocent *joie de vivre*.

Chan eil eòlas, chan eil eòlas
air crìch dheireannaich gach tòrachd
no air seòltachd nan lùban
leis an caill i a cùrsa.

There is no knowledge, no knowledge
of the final end of each pursuit,
nor of the subtlety of the bends
with which it loses its course..

In the long poem, '*An Cuilithionn*'/'The Cuillin', the poet's agitation is reflected in the fragmented and opposing meanings he attaches to the mountain. But at the end, the Cuillin rises '*air taobh eile duilghe*'/'on the other side of sorrow', symbolising the human spirit rising over adversity. The poem traces man's oppression of man, in Skye and throughout the world, in the present and throughout history. The ghosts of the perpetrators of the Clearances appear in a demonic dance on the rocky pinnacles. The cries of the people cleared off the land are heard. The Cuillin responds, rocking and shrieking on its torn bedrock. Men like Christ and Spartacus, who have sacrificed themselves for their people, are seen strung up on the hill. The Cuillin becomes a castrated stallion, the bogs representing the spreading of corruption throughout the world and the drowning of every honourable initiative. But the human spirit bursts forth; the Cuillin becomes a stag, lion, dragon, eagle. In the night on the Cuillin, in the darkness of despair, MacLean sees the human spirit, aspiring to what is unreachable.

Cò seo, cò seo, oidhche chridhe?　　Who is this, who is this in the night of the heart?
Chan eil ach an nì do-ruighinn,　　It is the thing that is not reached,
an samhla a chunnaic an t-anam,　　the ghost seen by the soul,
Cuilitheann ag èirigh thar mara.　　a Cuillin rising over the sea.

His poems are studded with place names. Thirteen places in Raasay are mentioned in the poem 'Hallaig'. Even for those who do not know these places, their names work at a symbolic level, showing they have been significant to people. MacLean's evocation of a populated Raasay does not stop there. His love and knowledge of the place allow him to hold a vision of the trees transformed into people, the native rowan, hazel and birch transformed into bands of young girls. This rises from a pre-Christian concept of the earth as an entity from which all life springs, to which it returns and then rises again in an endless cycle. So, though Raasay was largely cleared of its people in 1851, our enduring vision need not be of the present, time need not be linear. The poet's vision of Raasay is better than reality ever was, for he sees every generation simultaneously.

Soluis
'Lights'
reproduced by kind permission
of Carcanet Press Ltd

Chunnacas na mairbh beò.   The dead have been seen alive.

MacLean's poetry is largely pessimistic but is made uplifting by his belief
in the eventual triumph of human courage. The heroism of the heights is
contrasted with the low mean path he felt he had taken himself, especially
in his compromised response to the Spanish Civil War. Acting with conviction,
for better or worse, would have given him the integrity which was as much
a part of Gaelic heroic culture as of modern existentialist thought. In heroic
culture, the hero's leap of self-sacrifice combines conviction and deed; in
existentialist thought, an individual's leap of faith in claiming a subjective
truth is the most we can achieve. There are moments in his poetry when
he makes such a leap, the striving stops, and he glimpses the eternal in
the transitory, holding it in a verse against 'the bedragglement of time
and temptation'.

Nuair tha mo bhilean air a gruaidhean   When my lips are on her cheeks
boillsgidh uachdarain ra-dhorcha,   the inter-lunar lords are shining,
mìle solas shìos is shuas ann,   a thousand lights low and high,
falt ruadh is sùilean gorma.   auburn head and blue eyes.

This article owes a debt to what others
have written about MacLean, particularly
to John MacInnes, *The Poem Hallaig*
in *Calgacus 2*, 1975;
John Herdman, T*he Ghost seen by the Soul:
Sorley MacLean and the Absolute* in *Sorley
MacLean: Critical Essays*, edited by Raymond
Ross and Joy Hendry, Edinburgh 1986.

Soraidh Le Eilean a' Cheò

Màiri Nic a' Phearsain

with commentary by Anne Martin

Extracts from *Soraidh Le Eilean a' Cheò* taken from *Dàin agus Orain* by Màiri Nic a' Phearsain 1891.

Soraidh Le Eilean a' Cheò

Màiri Nic a' Phearsain

Soraidh leis an àit'
An d'fhuair mi m'àrach òg,
Eilean nam beann àrda,
Far an tàmh an ceò;
Air am moch a dh'éireas,
Grian nan spéur fo ròs,
A' fuadach néul na h-oïdhche,
Sòillseachadh an Stòir.

'Cur m'aghaidh air Glaschu,
B'airtneulach mo chéum,
'Cur mo chùl ri càirdean,
Nochd am bàigh cho tréun;
Ghluais ar buadhan nàduir,
Ann an gràdh dha chéil',
Shruth mo dheòir a bhàn,
Is dh'fhàilnich guth mo bhéil.

'S aoibhneach eilean Asgrab,
Fàilteachadh nan tonn,
'S uaibhreach creagan Gheàrraidh,
Sàilean fos an cionn;
Suas gu ruig th'm Fàsach,
Far an tàmh an sonn,
Stéin is Sgòrr a' bhàigh,
An t-àite 's àille fonn.

Seallaidhean bu bhrèagha
Riamh chan fhaca sùil,
Spréidh a mach ga'm fiarach
Madainn ghrianach chiùin;
'N uiseag air a sgiath,
Seinn gun fhìamh a ciùil,
'S an ceò mu cheann Beinn Dìonabhaig,
'S an sliabh fo dhrùchd.

Seinneadh gach fear-ciùil,
Le mùirnn a dhachaidh fhéin
'S cumaibh suas a cliù,
Ma bhios ur cùrsa réidh;
Ach cha ghabh sinn mùiseag,
Os ur cionn gu léir,
Nach 'eil spot is cùbhr',
Air an laigh driùchd o nèamh.

Translation courtesy of the
Màiri Mhòr Fellowship.

SORAIDH LE EILEAN A' CHEÒ

Farewell to
the Misty Isle

Mary MacPherson

Farewell to the place
Where I spent my youth,
Island of the high mountains,
Where the mist lies;
On which rises early,
The rose coloured sun in the sky,
Chasing away the night clouds,
Lighting up the Storr.

Turning my face towards Glasgow,
Sorrowful are my steps,
Turning my back on friends,
Tonight their affection is so strong;
Our natural talents surge,
In love all together,
My tears run down,
And my voice fails me.

Joyful are the Ascrib Islands,
Saluting to the waves,
Proud are the rocks of Geary,
With the woods above;
Upwards on until you reach Fasach,
Where the heroes rest,
Stein and Scorbay,
A place of very beautiful ground.

Sights more beautiful,
The eye could never see,
Cattle out grazing
On a Peaceful sunny morning;
The lark on the wing,
Singing with confidence, her song,
And the mist around Beinn Tianabhaig,
And the mountains under the dew.

Let all music makers sing with joy of
their homeland,
Boast of its fame,
its honour and dignity;
We don't mind,
we know that over all of you,
No place the dew falls on us,
can be more beautiful.

In 'Farewell to the Misty Isle'/ *'Soraidh le Eilean a' Cheò'* the Skye bardess Mary MacPherson writes of her profound regret for having to leave her native island and of the landscape images which would remain with her during her exile. One such is of the early rose-hued sunlight illuminating the Storr, a vista which she would often have enjoyed from her family home in Skeabost.

More than 130 years after these words were written, *The Storr: Unfolding Landscape* orchestrates a fundamentally different response to the same feature. The new work, with its *Soillseachadh an Stòir* (Illumination of the Storr), brings together two things which have anchored me through life, stayed with me as a constant, and inspired me on a daily basis: Skye's environment and the Gaelic song of its people.

The Storr is an icon of the multi-faceted and almost surreal landscape of Trotternish, drawing us into our surroundings, acting as a beacon on my regular journeys home. Countless artists have been influenced by its intensity and vibrancy. The Gaelic language lends itself to expressing both the beauties and cruelties of the land and its richness in this regard is revealed in the considerable works of Mary MacPherson.

Skye people know her better as Màiri Mhòr Nan Oran, which translates as Big Mary of the Songs, or simply by her patronymic, Màiri Nighean Iain Bhàin, or Mary, daughter of fair-haired Iain. Mary was undeniably a formidable lady who left a huge legacy of poems and songs which still retain their intensity, courage, pathos, beauty and relevance today. Born in 1821, she became heavily involved in the Highland Land Reform agitation during the latter part of the 19th century and used her poetry and song to give voice to her people and their environs.

Soillseachadh an Stòir

Sìne Gillespie

Soillseachadh translates from
Scottish Gaelic as 'enlightening',
gleaming a light from heaven.

1 From the poem 'The Woods of
Raasay', by Sorley MacLean
(*From Wood to Ridge*, p179)

The Storr. A bare pinnacle of rock. In a rocky landscape. Surrounded by
sea. The Old Man of Storr. A rock that has done time. A rock with a gender.
An ascent and a descent. The navigation of a mountain. But navigation is a
spiritual thing; it's about knowing who you are, where you have come from,
and what all of that means to you – to the soul that will one day fly from
your shell.

Skye is known throughout the world. The Gaelic explanation is 'winged
island'. An island that couldn't live up to its name without Trotternish – the
mother country of the Storr. The larger of Skye's two 'wings'. But although
it is 'Skye' which has survived, we know – if we like digging and scraping – that
the island had many other names too. If we go back two millennia, it might
be a humbling experience. Not only will we be dwarfed by the giant men and
women, but the entire island is named after shadows. Loch Scàbhaig in the
Cuillin country has opted to bear their burden, since it is 'the loch of the
shadows' – cast by the mountains and no doubt the mythical giants.

Skye is defined by mountains. The Trotternish ridge is the lava that spewed
out of the Cuillin hills. Some will tell you the Cuillin is named after the giant,
Cuchulain. Others will say to you that the real meaning is from the Gaelic word
cuilionn for 'holly', and the eye does see the prickly outline of a holly leaf, too.
But the myths frequently refer to 'the fire hills', and I like the simplicity of
that origin.

But the Storr wouldn't be half the man he is without water. Because it is the
patterns of rock and water and footprints that stir the porridge of poetry. It's
water that brought Columba, the 'dove of the church', to Skye in 685AD, and
his name is impressed all over Skye, in lochs, and churches, and islands. If you
suffer from depression, he's there to help too, since the herb, St John's wort, is
achlasan Chaluim Chille – Columba's armpit – to the Gaelic people.

Soil and soul combined are capable of great things. It is Skye's combination
of soil and soul that created *pìobaireachd*, the classical music of the Highland
bagpipe. Sorley MacLean speaks of 'the wood of Raasay in its gentleness, joyful
beside the Clarach' (in the Sound) as being 'the green variation on the pibroch
theme that the Cuillin makes with the waves'.[1]

2 The unique intertwining of the Gaelic
   landscape and its people.

3 The final line of the poem 'The Cuillin'
   by Sorley MacLean (*From Wood to Ridge*, p131).

4 From the poem 'Lights', by Sorley MacLean
   (*From Wood to Ridge*, p225).

The Storr does the work of grounding people. He is a fertile, triumphant symbol. The symbol of Trotternish. Watchman. Sorley MacLean burst from his husk. He stood alone with certainty. Spoke boldly of love and *dùthchas*[2] and oppression. A poet of conscience and courage. Rooted as well as international. Powerful, symbolic and truthful. This is the landscape that produced him and his lyrical cry went out into Scotland and the world.

On the Trotternish ridge, there is 'the pass that let out the shout', and – sure enough, a short distance away – there is 'the rock that heard the echo'. And, rising on the other side of 'sorrow'[3], 'a thousand lights'[4] were shining for Sorley MacLean. The Storr is just a bare masculine symbol. But the *'solais'* – the lights – represent the solace in his life that came from his marriage to Renee. Who heard his cry. Who became his earth.

It feels good to be digging. To be scraping and peeling away at this landscape of Skye. There is no Discovery, only a growing intimacy with the landscape, and a growing love of discovery. And so I discover that really there are hundreds of feet walking in my boots. Heritage is about doing time somewhere. With your eyes. Your ears. Your hands. Your feet. Your heart. Your soul. Your nose. And it's all intertwined in this thing called time.

The story of Skye takes in shadows and mist, fire and earth, air and water. The Storr explores what happens when those elements combine. We all know unity, and we all know separation. Everything is just a fragment in the end. Only God can see all the fragments, can comprehend how they all join together. But what's to stop us weaving our fragments into a thing of beauty in the meantime?

Tròndairnis
Meg Bateman

Tròndairnis

An seo chithear an talamh a' tuisleachadh,
chithear a chìr uaibhreach ga criomadh;
chithear slios na beinne a' sleamhnachadh,
ceum air cheum fad na slighe dhan chladach,
ceum air cheum dol fo uachdar na mara.

Thig daoine às a h-uile ceàrn
gus a' charraig chruaidh fhaicinn na ruith,
gus an saoghal fhaicinn mar staidhre bheò,
a' chinne daonna glacte oirr' an aon fhrèam a-mhàin,
is coltas air na ceumannan gu bheil iad nan stad.

Trotternish

Here you see the land lurching,
its frilled comb fragile;
you see the slope of the hill slipping,
step on step down to the shore,
step on step below the surface of the sea.

People come the world over
to see the solid rock in flux,
to see the Earth as an escalator,
mankind caught in a single frame
on steps that momentarily seem to stand still.

The Star

Alasdair Gray

A star had fallen beyond in the horizon, in Canada perhaps. (He had an aunt in Canada.) The second was nearer, just beyond the iron works, so he was not surprised when the third fell into the backyard. A flash of gold light lit the walls of the enclosing tenements and he heard a low musical chord. The light turned deep red and went out, and he knew that somewhere below a star was cooling in the night air.

Turning from the window he saw that no-one else had noticed. At the table his father, thoughtfully frowning, filled in a football coupon, his mother continued ironing under the pulley with its row of underwear. He said in a small voice, 'A'm gawn out.'

His mother said, 'See you're no' long then.'

He slipped through the lobby and onto the stair head, banging the door after him.

The stairs were cold and coldly lit at each landing by a weak electric bulb. He hurried down three flights to the black silent yard and began hunting backward and forward, combing with his fingers the lank grass round the base of the clothes-pole. He found it in the midden of a decayed cabbage leaf. It was smooth and round, the size of a glass marble, and it shone with a light which made it seem to rest on a precious bit of green and yellow velvet. He picked it up. It was warm and filled his cupped palm with a ruby glow. He put it in his pocket and went back upstairs.

That night in bed he had a closer look. He slept with his brother who was not easily wakened. Wriggling carefully far down under the sheets, he opened his palm and gazed. The star shone white and blue, making the space round him like a cave in an iceberg. He brought it close to his eye. In its depth was the pattern of a snow-flake, the grandest thing he had ever seen. He looked through the flake's crystal lattice into an ocean of glittering blue-black waves under a sky full of huge galaxies. He heard a remote lulling sound like the sound in a sea shell, and fell asleep with the star safely clenched in his hand.

The Star from *Unlikely Stories, Mostly*
by Alasdair Gray.
Reproduced by kind permission
of Canongate Books Ltd

He enjoyed it for nearly two weeks, gazing at it each night below the sheets, sometimes seeing the snow-flake, sometimes a flower, jewel, moon or landscape. At first he kept it hidden during the day but soon took to carrying it about with him; the smooth rounded gentle warmth in his pocket gave comfort when he felt insulted or neglected.

At school one afternoon he decided to take a quick look. He was at the back of the classroom in a desk by himself. The teacher was among the boys at the front row and all heads were bowed over books. Quickly he brought out the star and looked. It contained an aloof eye with a cool green pupil which dimmed and trembled as if seen through water.

'What have you there, Cameron?'

He shuddered and shut his hand.

'Marbles are for the playground, not the classroom. You'd better give it to me.'

'I cannae, sir!'

'I don't tolerate disobedience, Cameron. Give me that thing.'

The boy saw the teacher's face above him, the mouth opening and shutting under a clipped moustache. Suddenly he knew what he had to do and put the star in his mouth and swallowed. As the warmth sank towards his heart he felt relaxed and at ease. The teacher's face moved into the distance. Teacher, classroom, world receded like a rocket into a warm, easy blackness leaving behind a trail of glorious stars, and he was one of them.

(Ausgesetzt auf den Bergen des Herzens)

Rainer Maria Rilke

Ausgesetzt auf den Bergen des Herzens. Siehe, wie klein dort,
siehe: die letzte Ortschaft der Worte, und höher,
aber wie klein auch, noch ein letztes
Gehöft von Gefühl. Erkennst du's?
Ausgesetzt auf den Bergen des Herzens. Steingrund
unter den Händen. Hier blüht wohl
einiges auf: aus stummem Absturz
blüht ein unwissendes Kraut singend hervor.
Aber der Wissende? Ach, der zu wissen begann
und schweigt nun, ausgesetzt auf den Bergen des Herzens.
Da geht wohl, heilen Bewußtseins,
manches umher. manches gesicherte Bergtier,
wechselt und weilt. Und der große geborgene Vogel
kreist um der Gipfel reine Verweigerung.—Aber
ungeborgen, hier auf den Bergen des Herzens. ...

(Exposed on the cliffs of the heart)

Rainer Maria Rilke

Exposed on the cliffs of the heart. Look, how tiny down there,
look: the last village of words and, higher,
(but how tiny) still one last
farmhouse of feeling. Can you see it?
Exposed on the cliffs of the heart. Stoneground
under your hands. Even here, though,
something can bloom; on a silent cliff-edge
an unknowing plant blooms, singing, into the air.
But the one who knows? Ah, he began to know
and is quiet now, exposed on the cliffs of the heart.
While, with their full awareness,
many sure-footed mountain animals pass
or linger. And the great sheltered bird flies, slowly
circling, around the peak's pure denial.—But
without a shelter, here on the cliffs of the heart...

View to Raasay
Jony Easterby

next page:
Sorley MacLean
picture courtesy
of **Renee MacLean**

Special Thanks (continued)

Cathlin Macauley, School
of Scottish Studies Archives
Arthur McCourt
Donald MacDonald
& Aros
John Macdonald
Lord & Lady Macdonald,
Kinloch Lodge
Caley MacLean
Catriona MacLean
Renee Maclean
Midge Master:
A revolutionary patented abatement system
that continuously traps and controls Midge,
Mosquitoes and other blood meal insects
brought to you by the exclusive importer
of the Mosquito Magnet ®
Effie and Jan Nicolson
Morag Paterson
John Robb
John Phillips
Petzl Handsfee Lighting
Skeabost Country House
Sorley MacLean
(Somhairle MacGill-Eain)
Poet (1911–1996)
Staffin Youth Club
Alex Turner
Nicole Wallace
Whitewave

Warm thanks to our star
donors to date:

**'Grioglachan',
Ten Star Cluster**
Professor Seona Reid
'Causleen', Venus
Crispin Andrew Longden
The North Star
Chamberlain AMPR
**'Reul-an-iuchair, Ruaill
Mhor Sirius', Orion's Dog**
Podge Publicity
**'Caomai, Meadhan',
Orion, the Hunter**
GraphicalHouse

Stars:

'Grioglachan' The Pleiades:
Beerstecherhall Consulting
Cordelia Ditton
Stephen Flannery &
Michael Johnson –
in memory of Robert
McCann & Iain Coleman
Donald Fraser
Priscilla Gordon-Duff
Ralph Henderson
Jacqueline Lindsay
David Campbell McInroy
Elspeth McLachlan
Robert A Price
Peter Taplin
Peter Thierfeldt

**'Bogha Chlann Uis',
The Milky Way:**
Fiona Dick
Donald Fraser
Sheila Murray
Barclay Price

Sagittarius, The Archer:
Jim Jackson
Sheila Murray
Evelyn Tiefenbrun

Production Team

Jon Clarke
Production Co-ordinator
Duncan Grant
Site Manager
Dave Mason
Technical Manager
Jem White
Lighting Technician
Alberto Felisatti
Lighting Technician
Paul Gavin
Sound Technician

Crew

Neil Campbell
Lindsay Campbell
Ian C.Duncan
Dave Evans
Michael Gibbons
Murdo Gillies
Damien Hunter
James Jagger
DJ Macleod
Ewan Mackinnon
Alasdair Matheson
Robert MacGregor
Roddie McHugh
Ronnie Murphy
Graeme Steel
Stefano Tricanico
Paolo Tricanico

Front of House

Linn Leighton
Chris Leighton
Bryony Macdonald
Ann Marr
Sally Phelps
Ola Wojtkiewicz

Guides

Jamie Attridge
Bill Attridge
Elaine Caldwell
Bill Edgar
Nick Fellows
Sìne Gillespie
Sue Hamlin
Gill Houlsby
Gerlinde Krug
Chris Lea
Bridget Mackinnon
Ruari Mackenzie
DJ Macleod
Guy Matthews
Phil Moore
Neil Murray
Jon Pear
Gareth Ross
Angus Ross
Meike Schmidt
Micheal Speirs
Graeme Steel
Ian Tunnicliff
Stefano Tricanico
Chris Tyler
John White

Support & Review Group

Andy Anderson
Miriam Blain
Mary Carmichael
Alistair Danter
Les Downes
William Edgar
Jackie Gillies
Kati Kozikowska
Jack Lyons
Chris Lea
Anne MacLeod

Chrisanne McDonald
Donald MacDonald
Elsie McDonald
Kath McLeod
Rosie Somerville
Meike Schmidt
Sally Phelps
Sylvia Porter
Susan Reeves
Dugie Ross
Chris Tyler
James Wallace
Maggie Willoughby
John White

nva Board Members

David Arnold
Al Bell
Anne Campbell
Lisa Kapur
Stuart MacDonald
Shelia Murray (Chairperson)
Donald Reid

Special Thanks

Ken Abraham
An Tuireann Arts Centre
The Booth
Fiona Hampton
Bosville Hotel
Alistair Danter
Simon Fraser
GraphicalHouse
Claire Hannah
Margaret Hyde
Donald Kennedy
David Lloyd
Jaine Lumsden
Luath Press Ltd

Acknowledgements

nva would like to thank all contributors to the book and
the following people for their invaluable contribution
to *The Storr: Unfolding Landscape*

Creative Team

Angus Farquhar
Producer/Creative Director
David Bryant
Lighting Designer
Digger Nutter <slight>
Production Designer
Vicki Payton <slight>
Production Designer
Ed King
Construction Manager
Anne Martin
Performer/Researcher
Alex Rigg
Performer/Woods Sculptor
Geir Jenssen
Composer
Paul Mounsey
Composer
John Purser
Composer/Horn Player
Simon O'Dwyer
Composer/Horn Player
Ruari Cormack
Sound Designer
Gus Ferguson
Sound Editor
Jony Easterby
Original Sound Researcher
Dr Graham Tydeman
Forest Animation Designer

Somhairle MacGill-Eain
Original Recordings
Aonghas MacNeacail
Reader in English
Meike Schmidt
Reader in German
Sine Gillespie
Local Researcher
Cailean Maclean
Gaelic Language Consultant
Ishbel Maclean
Poetry Researcher

for nva

Ellen Gibbons
Executive Director
Katie Nicoll
Event Development Director
Nicola Godsal
Administrator
Sarah Wells
Financial Manager

Event Management Team

Caroline Adam
Project Manager
Kathy Hayes
Event Manager
Elspeth McLachlan
Development and
Marketing Manager
Adrienne Hall
Development and
Marketing Consultant
Clare Hunter
Community Liaison Officer
Jo Hunt
Environmental Consultant/
Planning Advisor
Jane Barker
Project Ecologist
John White
Hillside Safety Advisor
Pam Swift
Local Opportunities
Co-ordinator
Paddy Cuthbert
Podge Publicity
Ben Chamberlain
Chamberlain AMPR

the
STORR

UNFOLDING LANDSCAPE